GERRY DAVIS

# FLYING ON THE GROUND

The ups and downs of a career in the RAF and civil aviation

GERRY DAVIS

# FLYING ON THE GROUND

The ups and downs of a career in the RAF and civil aviation

**MEREO**

Cirencester

## Mereo Books

1A The Wool Market Dyer Street Cirencester Gloucestershire GL7 2PR
An imprint of Memoirs Publishing  www.mereobooks.com

FLYING ON THE GROUND: 978-1-86151-310-6

First published in Great Britain in 2015
by Mereo Books, an imprint of Memoirs Publishing

The address for Memoirs Publishing Group Limited can be found at
www.memoirspublishing.com

The Memoirs Publishing Group Ltd Reg. No. 7834348

The Memoirs Publishing Group supports both The Forest Stewardship Council® (FSC®) and the
PEFC® leading international forest-certification organisations. Our books carrying both the
FSC label and the PEFC® and are printed on FSC®-certified paper. FSC® is the only
forest-certification scheme supported by the leading environmental organisations including
Greenpeace. Our paper procurement policy can be found at
www.memoirspublishing.com/environment

Typeset in 10/15pt Bembo
by Wiltshire Associates Publisher Services Ltd. Printed and bound in Great Britain
by Printondemand-Worldwide, Peterborough PE2 6XD

# CONTENTS

Introduction and acknowledgements

# INTRODUCTION AND
# ACKNOWLEDGEMENTS

Having had the urge to write my memoirs of over 40 years working with aircraft, airmen and airlines, I was worried that my grasp of the written word was, to say the least, not up to the standard of a professional author. Looking at similar books confirmed that I had much to learn. The daunting task of completing this book could not have been achieved without the help of certain friends and relations, notably Peter Scott, Carmen Hart, Matthew Hart, Andrew Grant and Sam Grant. They have over time amended, suggested and offered advice, as well as supporting my amateurish attempts at telling my story. I am therefore indebted to them for their wonderful support, without which you would not be reading this.

I have penned these stories for my long suffering wife Lita, who during my RAF service endured much hardship, for my daughters, my grandchildren and my many friends. I hope you will enjoy reading of my experiences.

# CHAPTER 1

# IN THE BEGINNING

I was born around tea time, so my mum recalled, in the front room of our semi-detached house in Doncaster, on Friday 22nd August 1941. Dad wasn't present at my birth as he was away serving as a Flight Sergeant in the Royal Air Force, and on that particular day he was on attachment to RAF Drem, in East Lothian.

The Second World War was in full swing, and RAF Doncaster was a popular target for the Luftwaffe. Our house was just across the road from the station's grass runway, where many of the Dakota DC3 aircraft had come across from the USA to be prepared for distribution to RAF squadrons. This probably explains why, while she was pregnant with me, Mum decided to move house. That and the fact that the rent was cheaper for the three-bedroomed semi-detached house she moved into than for the four-bedroomed detached house our family had been living in.

With Dad away, when moving day arrived, Mum hired the milkman (I am assured he is not my dad!) and his horse and cart to help move our furniture and belongings. There was Mum, heavily pregnant with yours truly, and our milkman who just happened to have a wooden leg (a legacy from World War One), struggling to load all the items onto the cart. Fortunately it was a relatively short journey along the road to the new house and somehow they managed between them to offload all the furniture up four steep steps from the road to the house and get the wardrobes upstairs.

Mum often told me of the hardships she had to endure with Dad away, a young family and the shortages of both food and money. We didn't completely avoid the bombings. During one raid our house and those surrounding us suffered damage. The hot water tank burst and flooded the living room, several roof tiles were broken and the front windows were all cracked. This damage was never fully repaired during our remaining time in that house, as there was just not any money available.

To try and provide protection for us, Mum told me that during the early years of the war we had a small iron shelter erected in the front room, but this was later taken away for use in London — charming!

One of my earliest memories is of the Anderson shelter that was our 'garden shed'. I can still picture Mum doing her washing in there on Mondays.

To compound the hardship, not long after I was born Mum became very ill with suspected typhoid. I had two sisters, Ann (then two) and Marie (eleven). Marie, bless her, coped as best she could.

Years later I happened across a list of doctors' bills and fees for medication prescribed to Mum during her illness. This was an added financial burden as this predated the introduction of the National Health Service in 1948.

My first school was Beechfield Junior School, on Cleveland Road in Doncaster. It was a long bus ride away and a long walk to the bus stop; I was five.

One of my earliest memories of school was Mum buying me a violin and of me being enrolled in the music class. Perhaps Mum had aspirations for me to be a famous musician, but after a while the music teacher informed her that she was wasting her money as I 'could just not get it'. Truth be told, I wanted to be a footballer and I played whenever I could, often in plimsolls, as we could not afford proper football boots. I used to ask Dad for advice on tactics and such. This always culminated in him rubbing my legs down with the sporting page of the *News of The World*, which, he said, would make me a better footballer!

I still have vivid memories of the chastisement my dear mum used to administer to me. Boy did I get some leathering's when I was a kid. She used to hold one hand up high and smack both my legs at the back, not just once but at least a dozen times, even in public. When I could not control my outburst of crying and whimpering, she would warn me to stop, or I would get another hiding. I loved my mum very much, but I always seemed to be in some sort of trouble or other which necessitated a 'good spanking.'

Our next house move was for a two-year period when Dad was stationed at RAF Scampton in Lincolnshire as the Station Warrant Officer. This meant a change of school for me and I went to a junior school in the village of Dunholm, which again seemed a long bus ride away. Bizarrely, all I can remember about this village school was the foul-smelling outside toilets.

Initially we moved into married quarters, a hurriedly-erected prefab bungalow, but then we moved into a newly-built three-bedroom house, although we had to move out temporarily soon after as a tree-root burst through the floor of the living-room.

On returning to Doncaster, I went to Doncaster Secondary Modern School for Boys, in Danum Road, after failing my 11-plus.

My very first time wearing a uniform was as a Cub Scout. I

then progressed to becoming a full-blown Scout. Then, when I reached thirteen years and nine months, I joined the ranks of the Air Cadets, in the Air Training Corps (ATC).

My youth was very carefree. On Saturday mornings I went to the Gaumont Cinema, sixpence to get in, where I watched cowboy films and was entertained by many children's specialty acts, such as yo-yo demonstrations. In the cowboy films we saw Lash Larue catching all the baddies with his whip, Gene Autry, the singing cowboy, and my favourite, Flash Gordon. There was also Lassie the dog, and one series of films with a talking horse.

The afternoons were spent in the swimming pool (a pastime I continue to enjoy to this day), and then my pals and I went off to play in an old quarry, imitating what we'd seen on the silver screen. I also did a paper round to earn enough money to buy a bicycle with drop handlebars.

My reading material at this time was rather limited to comics, my favourites being the *Beano* and the *Eagle*, with Dan Dare, Pilot of the Future, a Spaceman Colonel, with his loyal batman Digby and his struggles and adventures with his arch-enemy, the green Mekon, who floated about on a sort of jet surfboard.

School, for me, was not very rewarding or fulfilling. There was lots of fighting, not only with some of the other lads, but with some of the teachers too. All the masters had nicknames, including 'Mary', the English teacher who would hit you with a ruler, 'Bomber', the geography teacher whose weapon of choice was a size 12 slipper and 'Pugh', the science teacher, who always seemed to be breaking the canes which were constantly in his hand throughout lessons.

Most feared of all though was the Headmaster. He had an immense office with a rack containing canes of various thicknesses. When you were ordered to his office he made you sweat for a whole lesson before inviting you in to bend over his desk, where you were awarded a minimum of six strokes.

Very often an emergency assembly was conducted in the large hall, for a public display of punishment by caning. One such public caning was meted out to the school's head bully, who had pinched the woodwork master's motorbike, ridden it around the playground and crashed it into a wall, bending the front wheel. He knew how to start it, but not how to stop it. He had a dozen strokes to his backside, and could hardly walk afterwards. He didn't cry though, and came off stage trying to laugh, boasting in a loud voice, 'It didn't hurt'. This gained him much respect amongst the other lads. Can you imagine the uproar nowadays if such punishment was dished out? Yet it instilled respect and discipline.

I got into a few scrapes at school, one for simply asking a girl in passing how her boyfriend who had left the previous term was getting on. Later that week I was told by my mates that the said boyfriend was waiting for me at the school gate. I guessed why he was there and there was no way of getting out of it. I entered the playground, where a large collection of supporters for both contestants awaited the coming fracas. No words were exchanged and we set to it. Thank goodness it was stopped by one of the masters before I got really damaged. I'm not altogether sure if I actually got a punch in, but he certainly did. My nose was bleeding, and after school I departed for home with two big shiners. I told Mum I had walked into a door. I'm not sure if she believed me, as thinking back I might have used this excuse several times.

I was subject to a public caning on one occasion, when I and some the boys were rumbled shimmying up a drainpipe, one at a time, to view the girls from the school next door (who used our gym) changing into their PE kit. Six lashes each for about a dozen of us in front of the whole school for that, but it was worth it!

We also managed to see off the odd teacher. We had a music master, but no one was the slightest bit interested in learning anything about music, including me. I had decided this years ago following my violin episode. His demise came near to Bonfire Night. On entering the classroom one day he was greeted with a hail of exploding fireworks, which not only scared the living daylights out of the poor soul, but resulted in our whole class being soundly caned in front of the whole school. Although six and a half foot and muscular, he never really got over the shock and left the school after suffering a nervous breakdown.

We got up to the usual sorts of capers that boys did in those days, using dinner money (if your parents could afford to give it to you) to purchase sweets or a single Wills Woodbine cigarette, to be passed around for a drag. Even gobstoppers were passed around for all to have a few sucks.

Gambling of sorts took place. In one game you threw either halfpennies, or if richer, pennies, against a wall. The winner was the owner of the penny nearest to the wall, but deciding who this was caused many arguments, resulting in fights. This game was also played for cigarette cards. These were in abundance throughout my school time. They had pictures of soldiers, trains or the like on them.

Some of the lads were from very poor families and wore hand-me-down clothes. Their footwear very often had holes in the soles and let in water. These kids had a bad time in the winter, not having warm clothing. I don't know how they survived with just a shirt and shorts in snowy weather.

I considered myself one of the lucky ones at school, having a father who had come through the Second World War alive and uninjured. There were not many in my class who had this privilege.

I left school without any formal qualifications, as did all the other boys. We left Doncaster when I was fifteen. My parents waited for me to finish school, but they had already decided we were moving to Bristol. Dad found it difficult to settle into civilian life after his RAF service and eventually secured work in Bristol with the engineering firm he had first worked for before joining the RAF at eighteen. The company was a small family concern in which several of his relatives worked, called Birds Engineering. It has long since disappeared.

In advance of the move we had previously journeyed by train to Bristol for Dad to look into the prospect of employment and find a suitable home. We would stay with Dad's sister during these visits. She had two boys around my age, and my cousins thought it would be good fun to provoke me because of my Yorkshire accent. I thought this odd, as I just could not understand their Bristolian twangs.

The provocation came to a head one day in the local park, where I took it upon myself to teach these two a few Yorkshire lessons in fist management. They went home crying to their mum and dad, telling them I had attacked them for no reason whatsoever. I got a real telling off, something by this age I was used to. Dad later pulled me to one side and told me how chuffed he was that I had thrashed these two.

When we finally relocated to Bristol and he started worked at Birds, I remember thinking it odd that Dad, an administrator in the RAF who had always been very smart and had advanced quickly through the ranks to Warrant Officer, was now working in a smelly factory. He worked as a vertical lathe operator, coming home daily in overalls covered in smelly grease and grime.

Seeing Dad looking smart in his uniform and seeing the activity and excitement at RAF Doncaster had obviously made a big impression on me, as I had already made my mind up what I wanted to do on leaving school. I got hold of all the information about joining the RAF Boy Entrants. I wasn't clever enough for the RAF Apprentices but managed to scrape through the Boy Entrants' entrance exam.

After a month in Bristol I set off for a life in the Royal Air Force which was cram-packed with adventures, and lasted for the next fifteen years.

I was five before I met Dad for the first time on his return from the war. After being posted to India in 1943 he returned home on the 13th October, 1946, having also seen service in Burma. Apparently there was some trouble with the Japanese tourists and he was sent out there to sort it all out. Well, that's what he told me!

Before I left home for the RAF at fifteen, Dad spent much of the interim 10 years away with the RAF. It was only when I was thirty and I had left the RAF myself that I had the opportunity to get to know him. I respected him greatly, and miss both him and Mum to this day. I often visit their joint grave to keep it neat and tidy and update them on how things are these days.

I used to ask Dad about his service career, especially about some of the incidents he witnessed while in the RAF as I have said previously he was a big influence on my decision to embark on a career in the RAF myself.

He joined up in 1928 as an Aircraft Hand General Duties. He and a pal had run away with the aim of finding a better life and they saw an advert for the RAF. The opportunity to get away from cramped living conditions with his nine siblings was undoubtedly a factor.

He told me that on joining the RAF he was astounded to be issued with so much personal kit, even underwear, something entirely new to him. Furthermore he had regular meals. But what really topped it off for him was that he had his own bed, unlike at home where he had to share.

Amongst his issued kit were puttees and a cane walking stick, part of the 'walking out dress'. He also recalled when toilet rolls were first issued to the Forces. In those early days they were accompanied by instructions for use. Each sheet was stamped 'Government Property'. Airmen were instructed to use only three sheets at a time, the first one for scraping, the second one for wiping and the third one for polishing.

He also told me that in those days they didn't have service numbers, as they all knew each other. He also told me that a Pontius Pilot was on aircrew training at that time. I later established that his service number was 509369.

His first posting was to Mountbatten, where he met Aircraftman T. E. Shaw, known in a previous life by another name.

In 1937, as a Corporal, he came second in the .22 rifle shooting Nobel Challenge Cup at Bisley. I have the bronze medal he was awarded in a display cabinet, with his other memorabilia commemorating his RAF service.

During his twenty-five years in the RAF he saw service overseas at many outposts and stations, including five years in Egypt before WWII, where he said he lost his hair flying in aircraft with open cockpits.

One of his jobs was to administer to captured Japanese POWs and in Burma he was constantly on the move to forward airfields with the advancing British forces. Conditions were very tough there and he spent two separate periods in hospital with dysentery.

It was whilst he was in Burma that he was fortunate enough to meet up with one of his brothers, who was a Company Sergeant Major (WO11) in the 4th Battalion the Royal West Kent regiment. Unfortunately a short while after they met up tragedy struck when his brother was involved in a fatal accident, on 31st March 1945. As a passenger in a Jeep his hat blew off, and whilst he was getting out to retrieve it his Sten gun fell from his shoulder and hit the ground, and a burst of bullets went through him. He was 28 years old.

Dad's first posting after the war was to RAF Lindholme as Station Warrant Officer (SWO). He said it was quite chaotic at the station as it had been selected as a processing centre for aircrew awaiting discharge, and as you can imagine they were somewhat demob happy. Dad was tasked with finding jobs for them to do and also giving them daily drill, which after the hardships they had endured did not go down very well.

In 1947 he went from there to Scampton as a Station Warrant Officer (SWO). The Lincolns and Lancasters were still based there and the next year 30 B29s arrived. We briefly tasted life there in married quarters and I used to visit some of the airmen's billets on occasion to swap comics, until they found out that my Dad was the SWO.

One tale that sticks in my mind is an event he witnessed at Scampton. It was winter, the snow falling quite heavily, it was dark and he wanted to get home for his tea. He was stopped on the steps of the station headquarters (SHQ) by a very senior Squadron Leader, who was the Station Administration Officer (S.Ad.O), an old-timer from the Royal Flying Corps days and a real stickler for etiquette. He was pestering Dad about a rota for the guards around a crashed aircraft. As he was talking to him, what appeared to be a very young officer in flying boots, the collar of his greatcoat up and hands in pockets, trudged past and nodded his head in recognition.

Well, the Squadron Leader went bonkers. He told my dad to go after him and get him to come back and salute him. Dad duly obliged, dashed off and asked if he would mind coming back and having a word with the S.Ad.O.

The young officer came back, covered in heavy snow, and asked 'What's up, old boy?' At this the Squadron Leader nearly burst a blood vessel, and shouted 'Shouldn't you salute a Squadron Leader when you see one?'

The young officer said 'Not since I was promoted to Wing Commander' and walked away.

Dad also told us that on each of his postings as the SWO to the RAF stations Lindholme, Scampton and Bawtry, it was his responsibility to check out all the pubs in each locality, to ensure their suitability for use by all the ranks. He was also to keep visiting each 'local' in turn, in case they were to be removed from the list. You can't make tales like that up, can you?

Dad left the RAF in April 1953. Due to reorganization within the service he was told he needed to apply for another trade, and in light of his experience as a drill instructor and disciplinarian it was suggested to him that he would be suited to the RAF Regiment. This and the fact that he might have to lose a rank or two was abhorrent to him, so he elected to leave the RAF when his contract ended and take his pension.

The first three years after leaving the RAF in 1953 proved quite a struggle for him as he adjusted to civilian life. He had a series of jobs which were totally unsuitable, until eventually in 1956 he and Mum chose to up sticks and move to Bristol, where dad originally came from and employment opportunities were more plentiful.

During his RAF service Dad was a bit of a gambler. He played a lot of cards whilst on the troopships and when on a lucky streak would often send some of his winnings home to Mum.

In his later years he was still into card schools and cribbage groups. He also religiously did the football pools. His greatest passion however was betting on the horses. I later found out through my daughters that when he offered to take them to the sweet shop this was code for 'I'm off to the bookies', and a quarter of pear drops secured their silence!

Dad passed away in September 1978, aged 68.

# CHAPTER 2

# BOY ENTRANT

~~~~

On moving with my parents from Doncaster to Bristol I immediately found myself in unfamiliar surroundings, not knowing a soul in my new adopted city. This feeling was to last for the next 15 years, throughout my RAF service. What probably made it bearable however was the excitement of knowing I was already in possession of my travel documents, a railway warrant, which had been sent to me by the RAF authorities. The warrant had even been amended to reflect my new departure railway station – Bristol Temple Meads. I noticed an initialled line had been drawn through the departure station of Doncaster, and Bristol Temple Meads inserted. It's funny how these small details are still vividly remembered, all these years later.

The day finally came, Monday 15th of October 1956, when I said my goodbyes to Mum, Dad and my sister Ann, and with great anticipation, excitement and apprehension, I got the bus to Temple Meads. I was clutching my few treasured possessions and some sandwiches my dear mum had made for me for the journey and departed Bristol Temple Meads via Platform One in a GWR steam train.

As if this wasn't a big enough adventure already for a 15-year-old, my journey to my new home at Cosford was not straightforward. I arrived at Birmingham Snow Hill Station and then found my way to Birmingham New Street for my next connection to Wolverhampton Low Level Station. From Wolverhampton I then caught my third train of the day to Cosford Halt Railway Station.

During the journey I noticed that there were other boys who looked a similar age to me and who were, like me, were also seeking advice as to which trains and platforms to take.

On arrival at Cosford a large group of boys, approximately 250 of us, assembled on the platform which, I remember to this day, offered commanding views of the RAF airfield. An RAF NCO gathered us together and we made our way to our first night away from the sanctuary of home to a new beginning and the start of many years of adventures.

There was no time to pause for breath or familiarize myself with my new surroundings, as the very next day consisted of a series of medicals, knowledge and aptitude tests designed to match us to a suitable trade within the RAF. I'm not sure of the outcome of the tests but it's fair to say I had one choice of trade. I was selected to be trained as a Supplier II, which meant absolutely nothing to me. We were also told that our entry group would be designated as the 29th Entry.

The excitement continued during this first week, as we were also kitted out with uniforms, underwear, shirts, boots, webbing equipment and a lot more, and given a large kit bag to put it all in. Kitting out was done in an orderly line but at great speed in a clothing store, where at each issuing point we were asked our individual sizes, which incidentally, nobody seemed to know, including me. This of course caused a lot of hilarity later when trying on the wrong-sized hats, berets, jackets and trousers. In fact we had our suspicions that this was some sort of ruse thought up by the issuing storemen to provide them with a source of hilarity.

Getting kitted out involved forming just one of the many lines we were asked to form during these first weeks. Another involved an introduction to the station barber. Although there were several barbers eagerly awaiting our arrival it was apparent that they only allocated one minute to each individual to relieve us of our cherished hair. The haircutting was frenetic, as you can imagine, and very quickly the barber shop floor was knee deep in savaged locks in a number of colours. This establishment would become a familiar destination over the following months.

The excitement kept on coming as, having been ordered to form a long line, we were each given a piece of paper with a set of numbers on it and told to memorize them, as these would be our individual service numbers. Mine was 1932824. This was followed by taking the 'Oath of Allegiance' to Queen and Country, and signing the Official Secrets Act.

That day I also had to take what was probably one of the most important decisions, if not the most important decision, of my relatively short life – how long I would like to serve. There were effectively two choices on offer. You could either sign on for nine years' adult service, with three years' reserve, or 12 years' adult service; this service as an adult would not begin until the age of 18. Whether this was a factor in my decision I'm not sure, but we learnt that from the age of 17 and a half we would receive the adult pay for the qualification rank that we had achieved.

For some inexplicable reason I selected the 12-year option. This decision, don't forget, was being taken at the tender age of 15 years and two months of age.

Our training as boys would last for an 18-month period, after which, on passing the final exams, we would be allocated individual postings among the whole of the many RAF stations throughout the UK, including Northern Ireland.

When the initial training started we were billeted together in our selective trade groups in wooden huts. This would last for a three-month period and we as a group of 29th Entry lads would serve this period in the Initial Training Section (ITS). The training mainly consisted of general service knowledge, service discipline and ground defence training, together with many hours of 'square-bashing'.

That parade ground certainly turned us green young lads into proficient, smart, obedient individuals. The introduction to our drill instructor corporal was an earth-shattering experience, particularly for those who just could not get the marching and the responsive speed to the level demanded. This overpowering, god-like individual would frequently unleash his repertoire of profanities (some I'd never heard of before) and insulting remarks, scaring the daylights out of most of us, which of course was his desired aim. It is fair to say that the discipline I had seen meted out at school was nothing compared to this.

It was apparent that the three-month initial training period was designed to sort out those individuals who, at such a young and tender age, had never experienced such a demanding, torturous and disciplined life and who had just possibly only recently disconnected themselves from their mothers' apron strings. Those of a somewhat timid disposition had, during that three-month period, the opportunity to opt out and flee from the rigors of this demanding training, which seemed relentless, and some did.

To add to our woes, during this initial stage in ITS we were, on many occasions, subjected to catcalls and goading from some of the senior entries, who on passing by us would refer to us as 'sprogs'. To compound matters further we were subjected to threats of what would happen to us when we finished this three month period and advanced up to the 'Fulton Block.'

Mercifully we did enjoy separate messing and we all ate together in the ITS Boy Entrants' mess. For some, RAF food was something of a culinary revolution and a sheer luxury in being able to select different choices from the various courses on offer, including a large selection of puddings, and on a regular basis too! Judging by the fact that some of the lads couldn't even hold a knife and fork correctly, this culinary experience was very far removed from their experiences at home.

Eventually the three months initial training was over and just before Christmas 1956, we were granted 96-hour leave passes. I returned to Bristol and delighted in showing my parents my newly-shaved head and my pristine uniform. I had previously sent my civilian clothes home. Some of the lads even took their entire kit home to show their parents.

Whilst I looked forward to the leave and the opportunity to see my family and update them on my adventures, this was somewhat overshadowed by the fact that I had the disadvantage of not knowing anyone of my age group in Bristol. At least I was able to make it home for Christmas. At this time there were roughly 2,000 lads training at Cosford and those who lived in Northern Ireland and other far-flung reaches of the British Isles, even with 96 hours of leave, were unable to make it home and back in time and therefore remained at Cosford.

I vividly remember the first part of my journey home to Bristol. We assembled at the railway station just outside the Cosford camp gates. A train arrived for the initial journey to Wolverhampton, where we would disembark and change trains and possible stations to pick up our onward connections home. The train to Wolverhampton was very crowded, and much bullying ensued. In some cases the senior entry lads relieved the younger lads of their leave money through forceful means, or just plain theft. I even witnessed some of the lads' kit being thrown from the train. I later learned that it was the kit of those lads who refused to toe the line, or roughly translated, who tried to stand up to the bullies.

On our return from my first home leave we had to experience the move into the Fulton Block, a large three-storey building containing in the region of 60 billets. Our allocated billet was on the top floor facing the parade ground. We had a new corporal drill instructor allocated to us, and he lived in a room opposite. There were 14 beds in the billet. Some were already taken by a mixture of other suppliers from the 27th and 28th entries. At the entrance was a room occupied by a sergeant boy from the 27th.

We sorted out our kit, made up our bed packs and tried to make conversation with the others, without much success, although we got the impression that a welcoming committee would later arrive to greet us, and we were right. In the evening we were visited by a large contingent of the senior entry, the 26th. All seemed to have painted entry sticks under their arms.

We were ordered to stand by our beds and they then proceeded to humiliate each and every one of us new boys, which culminated in all our kit and beds being thrown into a pile in the middle of the room. Some of the bullies even went a stage further than mental torture and were intent on causing physical distress. Three of them picked on the tallest of us new lads and, without provocation, proceeded to beat him up. Their motive was simple – it was to scare us, because they could, pure and simple.

Later that night, and for many other nights throughout our time there, the fire alarm went off. This of course meant that we all had to assemble for a roll call. It would seem that on each occasion when a new entry went up to Fulton block this happened. It also took place when an entry passed out and when another entry became senior entry. Or indeed when someone felt the need to disrupt the night's sleep and presumably get some sort of kick out of it.

What with the first night experience and subsequent episodes of bullying, fire alarms etc. I recall that many of us new lads did not sleep much during these first weeks in Fulton Block.

This also marked the beginning of our trade training. In preparation for trade training we were separated into our entry groups and marched off to the training rooms, where we were introduced to our new trade trainers, to learn about the timetable of lectures and the high performance levels they demanded of us.

On arrival back at the billet after a hard day's trade training it was quite common for some of the senior entry lads to try and order several of us to become their personal 'fags'. However this was not always accepted by some of us junior lads and would result in fights.

It was an extremely steep learning curve for me, as I hastily had to make the transition from an innocent young lad and adjust and adopt the harsh routines and discipline that were thrust upon us. Fortunately I did not suffer at the hands of the bullies as much as some and quickly learnt to keep my head down.

As well as the rigours of trade training it was also compulsory to participate in the numerous sporting activities on offer. These took place virtually every afternoon. Possibly my least favourite was having to run around the airfield over the three grass-covered hangars, which I recall was particularly exhausting. I did however like swimming and roller skating and much of the physical training in the large hangar-type gym, including wrestling. I tried boxing for a while, but getting hit a lot put me off, so I moved on to other less painful activities.

I recall that two of our number regularly volunteered for the exhausting runs around the airfield. However it later became apparent that this was not borne of a desire to get super fit but instead to provide an opportunity to burgle some of the local residents' houses. They were caught, found guilty of the offences, and dismissed from the service.

I managed to gain certificates in swimming and athletics which resulted in my being selected, along with my pals, to take part in the Wolverhampton Searchlight Tattoo and Cavalcade of Sports in September 1957. We were particularly excited about this as it was being transmitted live on the television. I still have a group photograph which was taken to commemorate the event. Needless to say, participating in these numerous sports resulted in our fitness being honed to tip-top condition.

When the next 96-hour pass was granted, to be honest, I was not looking forward to it. Whilst on my previous leave it had been good to see my parents, I did not know anyone of my age group in Bristol. So one of my pals, 'Taff', who came from North Wales, suggested that I accompany him home for this leave. He said that he too felt like some company from a friend during this time.

I wrote home to Mum and Dad to seek their approval and whilst I was upset that I wouldn't see them, Dad was very understanding. He had experienced the same sort of situation himself whilst he was in the RAF and duly wrote a letter authorizing his approval for me to spend time on leave with my pal. I've still got this letter.

Leave was then duly authorized and a railway warrant issued for the travelling to North Wales. I remember that Taff had a sister, who was a lovely girl, and thinking back now this may have somewhat influenced my decision to head to North Wales. I do recall however that we both had extreme difficulty in understanding each other's respective accents.

Our introduction to the rifle range had now begun. It took us a while to get used to the kick of the large .303 rifles (well, they seemed large to us – thinking back, some lads were only just slightly taller than the length of the .303). The rifle, if not held tightly into the shoulder, resulted in severe bruising of the shoulder blade. We quickly learned a practical use for our berets, which helped cushion the kick. As well as painful shoulders it also took some time to adjust to the noise of the explosion as the weapon was fired. Ear defenders were not available at this time.

As well as shooting the rifles, we were observed by the NCOs in the meticulous disassembling and cleaning of the weapons, which also later included the Bren gun. This repeated disassembling and cleaning ensured that we soon had this mastered.

Mealtimes in Fulton block were less enjoyable compared to our initial billets. Senior entries, of course, walked to the front of the queue. This was to be a privilege for when we became senior entry. But as they made their walks down the queue they revelled in randomly wrestling our mugs from us and then delighted in throwing them at a roundel painted on the mess wall and smashing them to pieces.

It was not just mugs however that were lost through acts of wanton vandalism. Outside the cookhouse was a large, deep, galvanized container full of boiling water; this was to clean your cutlery with. Many a lad carelessly lost their cutlery in the container, never to be seen again, but the senior entries got a kick out of throwing junior lads' cutlery in, just for laughs.

Weekends were often a welcome break from the intense training and routines. If you hadn't been confined to camp, on

Jankers or something else, Saturdays were free time. Some of the lads instigated liaisons with some of the many girls that seem to appear over the weekends. If you had the money you could go into Wolverhampton, in uniform of course. I often took the train to go to the cinema there, sitting through two or more showings of the same films.

I often visited the Salvation Army canteen for a bite to eat, but only if there was any spare cash left. I remember being on my own on one these sorties into Wolverhampton, and whilst on my way back to the railway station I passed a chocolate vending machine. So, as you do, I just happened to pull the lever and out popped a chocolate bar. As no one was about I pulled the lever again – bingo, another chocolate bar. On arrival back at the billet I was certainly popular with my pals, as I emptied my pockets, which were crammed full with chocolate bars, and passed them round.

As well as the option to continue to participate in the wide variety of sports on weekends you could, if you wished, join one of the bands and learn to play an instrument. This wasn't for me though. As far as I was concerned Saturday was a day off and an opportunity to experience the delights and excitement to be had in Wolverhampton.

Sundays were even better; marching to the compulsory church parade behind the superb bands, which included pipe, bugle, drum and bagpipe bands and drum majors throwing those large signal batons over the top of the central heating pipes which spanned the roadways and catching them to rapturous cheers. I really liked these occasions and enjoyed marching behind the bands, although it was not quite so much fun in the snow, ice and freezing winds.

On return to the billets we were released from duty, and if the weather was fine, we would pop along the road to a little café not far from the camp entrance, which was more or less a large hut.

This was of course only if you managed to negotiate the RAF policemen on the gate, who excelled themselves in bullying and inspecting your attire for the slightest infringement. If you did not meet their exacting standards they would take your details and send you back for the long walk to the billets to rectify the perceived problem. This was just another example of the many abuses of power which persisted where these acting corporals seemed to take great pleasure in exercising their power over us boys.

If you managed to make it to the café, one of the highlights was a juke box. Between us we would try and scrape together a threepenny piece to feed the machine and listen to the latest hits.

Another reason why Sundays were the highlight of the week was the arrival of the lunchtime train from Wolverhampton. This chariot of delinquency contained many dozens of young girls seeking adventurous liaisons with handsome, smart young lads… like me! So game were some of these girls that they often appeared during the week – well, so I was told!

This was a risky business, because, in contrast to a Sunday when we had free time, if you wanted to meet one of these girls you would have to exit the camp without permission. You would also have to break back into camp while hoping that whilst you were out having fun you had not been caught out by an impromptu roll call following a fire alarm, or even worse a snap inspection, which often happened. Some of course did get caught out, and some of the excuses proffered on these occasions were masterpieces of imagination.

The arrival of the Sunday trains with the girls even captured the imagination of one of the reporters of the *News of the World*. One weekend an article appeared complete with pictures of the girls alighting from one these trains. We were of course instructed not to form liaisons with these girls, some of whom were absolutely gorgeous, but as young lads, who was going to take notice of that?

We were specifically instructed not to hold hands or be seen attempting to taste the delicacies of their lip paint, but I am reliably informed that both of these activities were commonplace away from the prying eyes of officialdom!

As the months of training passed by we were subjected to three-monthly trade testing. On passing we were awarded a proficiency stripe and as we neared our final exams, we would ultimately end up with three proficiency stripes worn on the lower left arm.

As we progressed through our training and grew in stature and confidence many scams began to be thought up to fool those in authority. One of these was the 'Jankers' scam. Jankers was a punishment awarded for misbehaviour or some such other misdemeanour, which resulted in an attendance parade and being marched in before an officer. These punishments were awarded in days, from seven to 14, and meant being confined to camp and the withdrawal of all privileges. (One of these privileges entered in a little blue book could include permission to smoke.)

The more serious crimes could result in detention within the confines of the guardroom or ultimately, dismissal. Detention entailed assembling with others, with full kit, before and after working hours, in the presence of an orderly officer and sergeant. Attendees were allocated menial tasks, the most likely one being sent to the cookhouse NCOs to scrub a massive collection of pans and cooking pots which were congealed with grease and dried food.

The scam evolved from the realization that the orderly officer and sergeant weren't always those who had been a part of your training and therefore did not always know the boys who were serving the detention. So some boys finding themselves on this punishment duty would check out who was on duty and if satisfied they would be unknown to them, select a suitable candidate who would submit to their bullying attitude, effectively switching their identities.

Photographs on the old style RAF identity cards (RAF form 1250) could be shaved off with a razor blade, and attached with a bit of glue to someone else's ID card. The Form 1250 was checked on each parade by the orderly sergeant to verify that those present were the correct ones. The poor lad who had been forced to assume the identity of the offender would duly have his kit inspected, and if it was not up to standard, he would suffer the indignity of further charges being instigated. Fortunately for me, I never had to experience Jankers.

Pay parades were held on Thursday mornings and took up the whole morning, as there were so many lads to dish the pittance out to, about 10 shillings each. You had to await your name being called out and this was done in alphabetical sequence. My surname, it transpired, was shared by many others, so I had to listen out carefully for 824 Davis. 824 were the last three of my service numbers. Your name was shouted out by an NCO who accompanied the paying officer, and you had to respond with an equally shouted out, 'Yes sir!' as recognition, then march smartly along to the desk to salute the paying officer before and after receiving the money, and march smartly back to your position within the parade. You were closely watched during this procedure, and if your salute was not given in the smart manner demanded, you would be told to do it again, or possibly have to wait until all the others had received their pittances.

Alongside the parade ground was an old black hangar which had a corrugated pitched roof. Daubed on the roof were the numbers of earlier entries, some of which overlapped other previously long-departed entries. This graffiti was applied in secrecy at night, with stolen paint and bass brooms for brushes.

It's amazing that those lads managed this task, climbing up onto the top of this high building over the years without ever having a fatal accident.

Although we were growing in confidence and stature we were always, it seemed, at the mercy of bullying from the senior entry lads. Our billet was quite often used to carry out mock court martials. An unsuspecting individual would be selected and then spurious charges duly levelled against them. Despite his protestations, the individual to much hilarity, would always be found guilty as charged. A suitable punishment would then be handed down, with a popular sentence being made to push a coin or a washer along the room with your nose.

Another punishment was to force the accused onto a large wardrobe type locker and lock the door, kicking continuously against the outside and shouting that they were going to throw the locker out of the third-floor window. To add to the poor accused's ordeal they would physically move the locker through the room, kicking it continually towards a window overlooking a veranda on the same floor level as the billet. They would then cruelly throw the locker out on to the veranda, creating the illusion to the poor chap inside that he was indeed being thrown out of a third-floor window. The screams from inside the locker were ear shattering.

The bullying did happily subside when, as luck would have it, one of our number became a boxing champion. Not only was he in our entry, he was in our billet! It did take a few monumental scraps before finally word got around to keep clear of our billet.

In summer 1957, all the entry was dispatched by train to RAF

Woodvale, north of Formby, Lancashire, for the annual camp. Coincidentally I had actually been there the year before with the Air Training Corps from Doncaster. Days commenced with runs of several miles along the nearby beaches, followed by a multitude of activities.

Accommodation was in tents, and during the second week it rained a lot, so much so that my bedding and kit got soaking wet. I found myself shaking, shivering and feeling decidedly ill one morning, so I was carted off to the station sick quarters in an RAF ambulance and found myself a day or so later, when I awoke, in a hospital bed. I was the only patient and remained so for the whole week and a half I was there.

When I felt up to it I was ordered to get some fresh air, so I decided to explore my surroundings. At one point I found myself in an old garage housing a magnificent old car. I climbed through a broken window to get inside. Then I viewed the airfield to watch aircraft landing and taking off, especially a Spitfire which was based there. It took off each morning, on its way over the Irish Sea to gather weather information, coming back after a while to land safely. This was beautiful to watch.

After seeing the Medical Officer at the end of my recovery, he discharged me back to Cosford. I had to go to the station headquarters to get a railway warrant. Transport was arranged for me and my dried-out kit, a packed lunch provided and I made my own way back to Cosford. The others had already gone several days before.

My trade training as a supplier was well advanced by this time. A supplier is a posh name for a storeman, or in RAF parlance a 'blanket stacker'. As well as trade training we had education lessons, in English, Maths, Geography etc. I remember the Maths Education

Officer used to come into the classroom, set a subject for us to study and depart smartish, off somewhere else. You can guess what we got up to in these circumstances. It certainly wasn't studying.

One weekend, making a change from my frequent visits to Wolverhampton, a pal and I ventured off into the unknown countryside. We had no plan, but walked for ages along country roads seeking adventure. We eventually found ourselves in Shifnal, a small town about six miles from camp on twisting turning roads but only three miles away as the crow flies.

We managed to scrape together enough money for a tea and bun at a lovely little café. Unfortunately we were having such a good time that we lost track of time and realized we had not left enough time to re-enter camp through the normal entrance before curfew. We feared that on our return we would both be put on a charge for being absent without leave, so, after a short discussion, we decided we'd better get back as fast as we could.

We came to the conclusion that the fastest, most direct route would be to follow the railway line back to camp. So that's what we did, jumping from one railway sleeper to another. Fortunately there were no trains running at that time of the day.

It was very dark when we approached the outskirts of the camp near to where our trade training hut was located. We cautiously made our approach to the security fencing and proceeded to dig out a hole big enough to clamber underneath the fencing, which we eventually achieved. After brushing ourselves down, we both proceeded to march smartly through the camp to the billet. We made the lights out inspection just in time.

The time at Cosford for me and many others was a learning curve in life itself. Within a short period of time we were transformed from a bunch of young innocents into a smart disciplined group of airmen, something which I am proud to have achieved.

Fortunately I passed the final exams. This meant that from the age of seventeen and a half I would become a senior aircraftsman as a supplier II (two), together with what was to me a massive pay rise. On being told of this and after all the excitement, I was asked by our corporal instructor to wait behind when the others had left. He took me to one side and shook my hand, wishing me all the best for the future and telling me he was proud to have taught me.

There were a few of our number who actually failed the final exams. They were offered continued training by being relegated within the 30th entry for the next three months.

The next momentous experience was to be allocated our first postings. We had previously been invited to select an area of the country which we would prefer to be sent to. Mine was the West Country. It was a surprise to find out that I was going to be dispatched to RAF St. Mawgan in Cornwall. Where the hell was that?

We had the final passing-out parade. Throwing those rifles about in unison and keeping the lines straight whilst marching to the bands was for all of us a memorable, exciting experience and Mum and Dad managed to attend. After passing out we gathered our belongings together, made our goodbyes to each other, then proceeded on leave to start the next set of unknown challenges and stages of our RAF service careers.

I have, through the medium of the internet, been able to renew contact with five of my 29th entry colleagues. It's really rewarding to find out the chosen paths we have each undertaken in our passages through life to date. Some of the lads continued on within the RAF, attaining Senior Non-Commissioned status. Then there were others, like me, who left the RAF after completing their contracts.

There were those who chose to leave the RAF before their engagements were fulfilled, for a variety of reasons. I have also come into contact with several other ex-Boy Entrants from various entries, who also shared the camaraderie throughout both the boys' service and the RAF, of which I was privileged to have been a member.

So my service within the RAF begins. I have devoted a separate chapter to each of my postings. I do hope this journey through my service life and beyond will be an enjoyable read.

*Remember where you started from; remember how it was; the day that you departed, made you feel so down hearted?*

*The home you shared with siblings, Mum, Dad as well, was left behind and made you feel so lonely and so sad.*

*The distance to get there, by train or by car, was far from the comforts that you had seen so far.*

*You'd pledged yourself to serve your life, to train and learn a trade, as a Boy Entrant, now look what they have made.*

*The many of us that took this step do not feel regret. Those days of long ago taught us not to fret.*

# CHAPTER 3

# FIRST POSTING

## RAF ST. MAWGAN, 1958-60

⌒‿⌒

I arrived in the seaside town of Newquay in Cornwall from Bristol via a train change at Par, wearing my best blue uniform and clutching all my possessions in my kitbag. I had taken off my badges that marked me out as a Boy Entrant, although this was still my rank. I was now 16 years and 8 months of age. Little did I know that this was to be my home for the next two and a half years.

On arrival in Newquay, I sought directions to the bus station within the town. It was a fair distance along the road carrying all my kit. Along came a bus, a single decker. I got on and off we went along the winding Cornish country roads, about two miles to the camp.

I reported in at the guardroom and an RAF policeman directed me to the transit accommodation, where I spent my first night. I had to quickly find out where to eat and where to report to the next day.

This achieved, the next morning I made my way to the Station

Headquarters and reported my presence. I then had to notify all interested sections of my arrival by presenting myself with a blue card at each section. After I had given my details and signed the card I was then directed to the next section. This, as all RAF types know, happens at each new posting.

Eventually I reported to the Equipment Section Warrant Officer. He sent me onto the attached Technical Stores, where I was introduced to the NCO in charge, a Flight Sergeant. He was a rotund, fatherly figure who constantly smoked a pipe, blowing the smoke over everyone. The Flight Sergeant sent me off with an escort, a national serviceman, to get some bedding and find a bed in the billet occupied by others from the equipment section. It was in a WWII style rounded hut, which had been divided into two rooms by a wall across the middle. It had a stove in the centre. There were six beds in the room.

It was interesting to learn that I was more trade qualified than most of the other airmen in the section, which, I might add, rankled with some of them. Although qualified in theory, I had no practical experience whatsoever.

One of the billet occupants was a chap from the Emerald Isle. He worked in R&D (Receipt and Dispatch). Paddy was not bothered much by anyone, as it might have upset him. He had very few pieces of kit and those few bits he had were chucked about.

There were three civilians working in the stores, along with several national servicemen, a sergeant, a couple of corporals and a few regulars.

I was grateful for this type of work, as I had an unexplained hatred of working in an office. But being still a Boy Entrant, it soon became apparent that I had absolutely no experience in the operational activities of the stores. Yes, I had the qualification of Supplier II, but putting the paperwork into practical usage just wasn't there. I had another learning curve to climb.

There was also the added light-hearted response to my innocence in naming the NCOs by their proper titles, for instance Corporal, instead of what seemed the norm of corp, sergeant as opposed to sarge, and then flight sergeant as opposed to chiefy or chief. Sometimes this could get me into trouble, as those of the squeezed brain variety would pick on me because I was so young. This incidentally carried on throughout my service life.

The Technical Store was a large corrugated building, with an office attached. It had a stove in the centre and it became my responsibility to attend to the task of cleaning and refuelling it. This office was laid out so that the Flight Sergeant could oversee all that was going on. He used to get really agitated when some of the young aircrew sergeants kept coming round with spurious requests for items of equipment. Each visit was purely designed to chat up one or other of our WRAFs.

I recall that all I seemed to be interested in was messing about, especially when it came to stacking items which were placed high up. The shelves were laid out in rows of angle iron and were about 20 foot high. One time, while I was stacking items on the top shelf, a National Service lad and I were throwing things about when I got over cautious in throwing to him at that height and hit one of the fluorescent light tubes, which burst and showered both of us in a white powder. The flight sergeant made us both go to sick quarters for a check-up with the MO.

The Squadron Leader Section commander was an ex-Aircrew Officer. Obviously he did not engage in conversation with the likes of me or other airmen. He seemed to be suffering constantly with his eyes. It was also obvious that he had had plastic surgery. The story going about was that he had got injured about the face in a burning aircraft.

The other chaps in the billet gave me the job of 'coal and coke snatcher'. This was a task carried out once a week, after the fuel supplies wagon had visited each billet and dumped whatever was on offer into the coal bunker inside the billet porch. Sometimes it was coal and others it was coke. I had to get down to the billet sharply, bag up what had been delivered, place it in the billet and lock the door. It was also my responsibility to try and thieve other billets' fuel, if I could, without being seen. These fossil fuel burning stoves were very temperamental. If you were not careful all the fuel could be burnt up in a few hours. Another skill to master!

The national servicemen in the section took great delight in telling me what a stupid fool I was for signing my life away for 12 years at such a young age. Well, actually in my case it was 15 years. All these lads had demob charts, both in the section and the billets, and they constantly reminded those of us regulars of their remaining sentences. Sometimes this was done in a singing voice or even on occasions, in verse.

There was a diverse collection of very qualified people amongst them, some of whom were even more educationally qualified than some of the officers. One of these lads, who I became very friendly with, had completed an apprenticeship in carpentry, which he was eager to get back to.

Eventually I reached a turning point in my career. I got to the magic seventeen and half years of age. My pay then went up from one pound 10 shillings a week to three pounds 10 shillings, an absolute fortune to me. Also my name was promulgated in station routine orders, informing all and sundry that I had been promoted twice on the same day, firstly to Leading Aircraftsman, then to Senior Aircraftsman. This was received with astonishment by many who thought I was a lowly young sprog. Well I was, wasn't I?

I kept up the payment to my mum of a shilling a day. This continued throughout my service, until I got married.

The set of lads that I had the privilege to befriend all had motor bikes, so now the time had come to buy one myself, as I was a bit miffed at being the pillion passenger all the time. After all I was now rich enough to afford one. I gingerly approached my dad to seek his support in acting as my guarantor on the hire purchase form. I raided my Post Office Savings (POSBY) account for the deposit and purchased an AJS 500cc single cylinder motor bike. This was later changed for a Matchless G9 twin 500cc model. I had to register the vehicle with the guardroom and they allocated me the number 400, which had to be displayed on the bike.

Not long after this I applied for my driving test, as I was very sensitive about the 'L' plates, and just wanted to grow up fast. The test day came through the post and on the appointed day, off I went to Bodmin to take it. Surprise, surprise, I passed. Was I chuffed!

This then gave me the freedom to join in with the rest of the lads, about a dozen of us, who on every occasion that money would allow toured all over sunny Cornwall, mostly at weekends, visiting anywhere there was a dance or a festival or a gathering of 'totty'. Blimey! Plymouth (in Devon) was the place. There was a Forces Club, and at the entrance a large collection of female predators waited, of all age groups. As soon as they clapped eyes on you, they pounced and grabbed you, and wouldn't let go until they got inside. That was when some of them disappeared and made a beeline for an unsuspecting matelot, or you might even get lucky yourself!

Matelots were in bigger demand in Plymouth than us 'Brylcreem Crab Fat' boys. On one of these occasions the girl I took in said it was something to do with 'staying power', Whatever that was! Ladies were not allowed in unescorted.

Very often on exiting camp on our motorbikes we would be stopped by an RAF policeman, who would insist on checking our vehicle passes. There were also occasions when a sample of fuel would be taken, to see if it was RAF petrol.

One day I decided to go to the pictures in Newquay, with my mate Taff on the pillion. The light was starting to fade and my lights were on. When I got alongside the Bristol Hotel, the manager of this establishment, driving a black Rover 90 from the other direction, turned in front of me, causing me to crash into the passenger side of his car. My passenger flew over the top while I tried to go through it. That was the last time I rode a motorbike! I finished up in the local hospital for a few days, after which an RAF ambulance came to collect me and delivered me to Station Sick Quarters. I received two broken teeth and a gammy leg.

Whilst I was in the Newquay hospital a gorgeous nurse attended to me (I looked her up when I was better). She was keen on furthering her career in nursing, so I reluctantly gave her a hand with her training, mostly in how to administer the new system of mouth-to-mouth resuscitation...

Then whilst I was in the station sick quarters, in bed and unable to walk and clean my face properly, I was visited by the Medical Officer, whose only interest in my ailments was to chastise me in an aggressive, authoritarian way. He ordered me to get a shave. I was glad to leave sick quarters. It gave me an unhealthy feeling.

Can any of you remember the RAF shirts that we wore in those days? The ones with the detached collars, attached with front and back studs, which used to mark and dig into your throat and neck? They used to go to the laundry for cleaning and starching. I was still growing at the time and the thought of having to buy new shirts and collars just did not enter my head. This was attributed to the fact that if I had not spent my £11 yearly clothing allowance, it would be paid to me. These were the days when I would only spend any of this allowance if I was ordered to.

Laundry was sent in weekly, wrapped in a towel, and boots and shoes always seemed to wear out quickly. Both had to have labels attached, with name and service number clearly visible. Gosh!

When shirts first arrived with attached collars, you had to buy them. No, I did not buy any, but I looked eagerly at those who could afford them. It was much later that they became standard issue. These were the days when I only had one 'civvies' shirt, which I used to attempt to wash, then wring out and put on, hoping that it would dry by the time we got to the first pub.

I met and teamed up with another ex-Boy, who had been trained at RAF St Athan. He had been trained in the 30th Entry. He also came from Bristol, so that was two things we had in common. He was originally posted onto 42 Squadron 'Shackle bombers' (Shackletons) at St. Evel, which was just up the road from St. Mawgan. This base was closed down in 1959 and all personnel and aircraft came to us at St. Mawgan. They even brought the WRAFs with them. St. Mawgan didn't have any before this. Incidentally we two are still the best of mates today and meet regularly. His trade was 'Honey Cart Emptying Executive', or as sometimes referred to, an 'Airframe Fitter.'

He of course had a motorbike at the time, and he seemed to have great regard for hedges. I mean I always followed behind him on my bike, so that I could fish him out of the latest hedge he had driven into. We had all these hedges marked on a map, but due to the roads being improved, all these sites have now been removed. I still manage to take the p**s out of him though, whenever we pass nearby these spots. His initials, by the way are VD.

I witnessed two separate aircraft crashes. Both were Mk. 3 Shackletons on their delivery flights and in both cases their nose wheels collapsed on landing.

BOAC had taken delivery of their new B707s and were doing their crew continuation training at St. Mawgan. Well, it came to pass that a brand new system of stores delivery had just started, called 'Forward Supply'. This was to save tradesmen from wasting time going to the stores and collecting items. Guess who volunteered for the job?

During one of these deliveries to 42 Squadron's hangar and technical facilities, where all my mates worked and on occasions got their hands dirty, the BOAC crew shared their crew room. I asked the Captain of the 707 if I could have a flight. 'Yes' he said. So I asked the driver of our three-tonner if he would wait and take me back to the section, thinking that it would only be a half hour or so flight. We took off. We didn't land again for seven hours.

I was worried to death in case I was going to be charged or court martialled for being absent from place of duty, or something. But when I got to work the next morning, honestly, no one had missed me!

My mate Tiny (the ex-30th boy) pushed the steps into the aircraft on landing, and met me. He was also worried. He had gone over to the Motor Transport (MT) section earlier in the day to fill up the tractor with petrol, putting in about 20 gallons. He then drove it back over to his squadron, which was a fair distance there and back, and as it was lunchtime he got the transport to the airmen's mess for a spot of grub.

When he got back to his squadron all the fuel had been siphoned out of the tractor, presumably for use in individuals' cars and motorbikes, and his Master Technician boss (Warrant Officer) demanded to know from him why he hadn't filled it up.

I got to work one fine morning and the Chiefy (Flight Sergeant) told me to report to the Station Warrant Officer (SWO). When I got there I was surprised to see a dozen ex-Boys gathered. The SWO briefed us, informing that we had all volunteered for a funeral parade for a deceased flying officer who had been killed in a car crash. We practised .303 rifle drill, which of course impressed the SWO. After all, we were all ex-Boys.

We were driven to the (now famous) St. Evel church with our three blank .303 cartridges and rifles. The bullets were tucked into our webbing belts. I lost one of them in the churchyard, and had to do a pretend job for the last shot. Over the years I have revisited this lovely church many times and I still haven't found the bloody thing! One of our ex-Boy biker pals lies at rest there, next to the Flying Officer, after a fatal motorbike crash.

The chiefy ordered me to attend the education section and enlist for further qualifications. I thought I had enough certificates, and didn't want to go. But hey! The classes were full of WRAFs, so I kept going and made lots more friends, some of whom were very attentive and attractive. After all, I needed assistance in helping to understand some of the difficult mind blanking things I kept getting!

In those days Newquay in the summer was full to overflowing with tourists. The winters were something different. The place was like a ghost town. The pubs depended on the RAF keeping them going. There were occasions when a falling out with a publican arose and the word soon got around to the thousands of RAF lads and lasses to boycott them. It was a bit different from today's Newquay, with no servicemen and plenty of holidaymakers (especially Australian surfers) throughout the year.

Station duties were a bind. There was fire picket and armoury guard. I was doing one of my stints in the armoury with these two other guys, who happened to be mates. It took two to open the double security doors. For some reason they insisted on enlightening me on how to overcome this system so that one person could achieve this task alone. I wondered why, and soon found out.

The orderly Sergeant and the orderly Officer came for their check about 1930 hours. One of the lads asked if they were coming again that evening, as they wanted to get their heads down early for the night, because they had an early start at work the next morning. The Orderly Officer said that as a result of this, they wouldn't bother to visit again that night. Well, as soon as the two had gone, these two mates departed sharply off to the NAAFI (Navy Army Air Force Institute), leaving me on my lonesome, which was not allowed. They got back much later with a skinful of ale inside them.

Now you may have gathered that for us young (very young) airmen that our testosterone levels were exceedingly high. Something in the local water?

I had this friend (you have probably said this to your doctor at some time or other) who explained it thus: imagine you are a racehorse. A stallion, if you like. They don't always have the same jockey; everyone wants a ride, what more can I say?

We bikers used to have competitions. Off we would race to a pre-selected destination, and arrange to meet in a pub, café or somewhere. Our objective was to see who could score the fastest and bring a lady into the premises. Only acceptable totty counted. You just would not believe how many times our record was broken.

The highlight of the month was the camp dances, very popular events. Loads of buses came, bringing what seemed like the entire female populace of Cornwall. These were held on Saturday nights. There was always a mad rush for the bikers to get their machines out of the billets, and to try and make them less smelly, this was to provide some sort of accommodation for the several stranded ladies who had somehow missed their buses home and accepted the generous offer of a bed for the night.

It was always a source of amusement to me and others to see these ladies and their escorts dashing up between the billets, first thing on the Sunday mornings, going to the toilets. Shortly after several motorbikes would shatter the morning's peace, starting up their engines and departing with these ladies to help speed up their departure to whence they came. Several of them, I was reliably informed, were married to servicemen who were abroad.

Then all of a sudden, the expected notification for a posting abroad came. It would seem to ignore all the selections I had asked for. It was to Aden, just the place I did not want to go to. But there you are. That's life!

# CHAPTER 4

# RAF BAHRAIN, 1960-62

~~~~~

My heart melted. Some bright spark at RAF Innsworth (where all RAF personnel were allocated their postings) had selected me for posting to RAF Khormaksar in Aden. My journey started from Bristol, on the 1st September 1960, via Temple Meads railway station to Swindon. I was met on the platform, with many others, and bussed to a transit camp called RAF Clyffe Pypard, in Wiltshire. There we were issued with bedding, which we carried for a long walk to a freezing cold wooden billet. A fire was soon lit in the stove positioned in the middle of the 30-bed room. There was not enough fuel to keep it going all night – typical.

After an early breakfast the next morning a busload of us travelled to RAF Lyneham, where we boarded a Comet MK2 for the first part of our journey to RAF El Adem on the Northern Coast of Libya, near Tobruk, a place I was to visit many times in years to come

On landing at RAF Khormaksar, I was again allocated 'luxurious' transit accommodation and settled in. The next day we were met by the Station Warrant Officer (SWO) who lined us up and inspected our khaki dress uniforms. We were all given the usual lecture about not altering them in any form from the original issue. Just about everyone shortened their shorts, as most of the issue ones came to well below the knee.

He then came up to me and asked my name, and I told him. He then scared the pants off me by informing that he had selected me to report to the Station Commander's office the next morning at 0900 hours.

Well, I can tell you, I was scared. I had never been near a Group Captain before. I did not sleep much that night, and spent a lot of the time getting my kit ready and worrying. Why I had been selected and what was I going to have to do? Nobody was willing to help me desert. I could not escape to anywhere. Mum, where are you?

I made sure I was not late, missing out breakfast, too scared to eat anything. I reported to the Station Commander's office in the station headquarters and his PA, a Flight Lieutenant, told me to enter. Wow!

I saluted and stood stiffly to attention. He asked my name and told me he was going 'up country' for a couple of days, and wanted me to answer his phone and take his messages.

What an experience that was. I was literally scared stiff all the time. I ran out of paper writing down those messages, and I didn't know where to look for some more.

On being released from this nightmare task three days later, I was told to report again to the SWO to be given another task which, he said, was of great importance. He most graciously instructed me to walk around the domestic side of the camp with a plastic bag and pick up paper and other rubbish.

I was at Khormaksar for about ten days, having to complete

many menial tasks that were allocated to me and others in the same situation. All were awaiting information as to where we would finish up. By this time I had found out that there were several other outposts and stations which I could be posted to within the Middle East Air Force command. I had no idea what was to come.

Eventually, several of us 'transited' airmen assembled to be informed of our postings. When it was my turn, I gasped at learning that I had been chosen by a select committee of general office bods for a posting to RAF Bahrain. Where the hell was that, I wondered.

RAF Bahrain, as it was then called, was situated on an island called Muharraq, accessed over a causeway from the main Island of Bahrain. The runway traversed the whole island (RAF Bahrain's name was subsequently changed to RAF Muharraq.)

My arrival at RAF Bahrain was something of a shock to one of my young years. The heat, for a start, was indescribable and took some getting used to. Come to think of it I don't think I ever did.

Going around with my blue arrivals chitty I found that I was not going to the stores, but to the Air Movements Section. Why there, I wondered? I was soon made aware that it was an offshoot of the supply trade, of which until then I'd had no idea. This staging post, at that time, had a complement of about 400 RAF personnel. So I started my eleven years' service as a 'humper and dumper' in a totally different trade from the one I had been apprenticed to as a 'store-bashing blanket stacker'.

I had quite a lot to learn. I found it interesting and felt that working on transport aircraft had put me at the forefront of the RAF's work. There was a lot of different paperwork to master, including aircraft weight and balance sheets, some of which were huge documents on which a graph of the balance of the aircraft's trim had to be configured and drawn, together with the weight and distribution of the cargo and passengers. There was much, much more 'on the job' training to pick up and glean from the other lads, officers and NCOs.

I was allocated a billet – Block 18. To my surprise I noted that I was sharing a large room which contained 90 beds. There were two rows in the middle of the room and beds along both sides and both ends. There was a large air conditioner fixed to a side wall in the centre of the room, which was on constantly, 24 hours of the day.

The ablutions were some distance away, and just outside the entrance door it stank to high heaven of urine. There were often power cuts, especially at night when all would be awoken, as the constant hum of the air-conditioning machine stopped and the resultant heat instantly struck each one of us with a vengeance.

Every couple of months a spraying of DDT took place in the blocks, as bed bugs, rats and flies were rife. With the doors locked and entrance forbidden, it was really hard for those of us who had just come off night shift, knackered and wanting sleep. Lying on a concrete patio for the flies to feed on me was not my idea of rest.

During these times the shower blocks were full of lads sleeping with the water on full blast (the water by the way was always at the outside temperature) to give some form of relief from the flies, the heat and that curse of deserts, 'prickly heat', a condition contracted in very hot climates which causes an itchy rash which can cover the whole body. Some relief can be obtained with calamine lotion. If not treated, it can result in open sores.

Some of the rats in the billet were huge. Seeing their footprints on your pillow in the morning when you woke was quite disturbing, I can tell you.

We had an Arab who came in daily to clean the place and make beds and cups of tea, which we had individually to pay for. Of course there were certain individuals who just would not pay him, even after promising to do so. This poor chap used to get quite upset over this.

There were occasions when an inebriated airman got himself into trouble with the local police. I recall this one chap, a telegraphist, who seemed to be getting his fair share of Jankers, and was not the favourite of his CO. It came to pass that after a rather large consumption of liquid refreshment, this individual, in the dead of night, took himself down to his CO's married pad, which was on the main island of Bahrain, and borrowed his motor. Having driven around the island until the fuel was nearly all used up, he drove it out onto the beach. The tide at Bahrain used to go out rather a long way, and he dumped it. On reaching terra firma, he then began to make a nuisance of himself amongst the local populace. The local police got hold of him and locked him up. It took a month to get him back!

During my second year there, we were surprised to see a chilled water supply being installed on the outside of every other billet wall. This had to be topped up daily with 20 gallons of fresh drinking water. This of course did not always happen, as it was the responsibility of the Arab employees of the Barrack Warden. I should imagine the powers that be were getting fed up of the cookhouse doors being bashed in at night-time so that raging thirsts could be sated.

The only thing was, there was an Arab village just the other side of the fence, about 100 metres away from the billets. Would you be surprised to learn that a large hole was cut into the metal fence so that the 'Bintas' could walk through and help themselves to our water, then carry it away in large pots on their heads? No wonder the tank was always empty. They incidentally had to buy drinking water. Eventually measures were taken to stop this happening, although there never seemed to be enough drinking water available.

Time off from work was spent in the pool, at the camp's Astra cinema, or wandering round the beaches, which stank of sewage and dead fish. The tide on the Island of Muharraq came in and out very quickly, which resulted in several Arab driven lorries getting stuck on the beaches whilst collecting coral for building.

Mail was very important. I wrote a lot of letters, as did most airmen. There happened to be a postal strike in the UK at one point. The postal service at overseas stations was organised by the Army Postal Corps. During this strike one of their lads had a mental breakdown due to the incessant personal calls to his depot and the phone calls from frustrated airmen, all blaming him for their lack of mail and the incessant questions as to when the next batch of mail would be received.

Occasionally we would get a visit from a Combined Services Entertainment Company (CSE). I have a photo of me standing next to Charlie Chester, who had just arrived with his entertainments troop, some of whom were exceedingly pretty.

Occasional trips to the capital city of Manama, for fact-finding purposes, were made. I used to accompany several of the lads, who would ask me to look after their coats whilst they visited some house or other. I don't know what this was for, but they always seemed to be smiling when they came out.

One time I witnessed a party of Arab prisoners shackled at the neck with chains, presumably on route to Devil's Island, just off the coast.

I managed to wangle a fortnight's leave down to Mombasa, in Kenya. I was amazed at what I witnessed of the goings-on at this busy African port. I was accompanied by an MT driver from Bahrain, who worked with us. We had a whale of a time. We went via a Beverley aircraft to Khormaksar and stayed in the Red Sea House, which incidentally was RAF servicemen's transit accommodation, loosely described as a hotel. I was placed on guard on the front door all night, with a .303 rifle and 15 rounds of ammunition, contained in a sealed box, with instructions from the guard commander not to break the seal under any circumstances...

We flew on to Kenya in an Argonaut aircraft of Aden Airways. On landing at the local airport of Kilindini, I was amazed to see this green stuff on both sides of the runway; I was later told that it was something called grass. I had forgotten what it looked like. After going through customs and a long bus ride through the Kenyan countryside, we were dumped off in the centre of town and told to enjoy ourselves.

On asking around we found that there were two hotels which specifically catered for forces personnel on leave. They were the Rainbow and the New Bristol. Being from Bristol, you can guess which I chose. It was of course run by an Indian gent. What an experience that was. The owner advised us to deposit all our cash with him and book out sufficient money for each day's adventures, in a sort of bank account, which we did. He informed us that all other servicemen did this and he could not be responsible for any thefts which may occur. This was Africa, remember.

I witnessed many unmentionable things whilst in Mombasa. Especially what soldiers and airmen on leave from desert outposts got up to. There was of course much drunkenness and fighting amongst the servicemen. But my stay there was a real treat, especially eating fresh food and eggs, which actually did not taste of fish, as they did back at base. The Indian owner of the hotel used to moan like hell when we demanded our breakfasts with chips, at two in the afternoon, when getting up from our beds from the festivities of the night before.

The two weeks were soon over and then it was back to our desert island, which took two days of travelling via four other desert outposts. On Friday 6th October 1961 a Blackburn Beverley arrived from Kuwait (Q8) at Bahrain; tail number XM 110, loaded full with several tons of boxed live 105mm howitzer cannon shells. It was nearly lunchtime and we wanted to get off so as to avoid the mess queues, and leave the offloading until later. The boss decided otherwise, because it was ammunition! At this time one of the many 'practice' war exercises was under way, so we offloaded it rather sharpish.

As we were ambling back to the section and we were about a dozen feet away from the aircraft, when there was an almighty explosion. The aircraft had blown up. It later transpired that a bomb with a timer had been placed on board at Q8. Wasn't it fortunate that it did not go off when the aircraft was airborne, or when we were on it? From then on all the Arab workers were excluded from the camp. Work from then on became that much harder.

I got promoted to Corporal, and Mum and Dad were pleased.

Our boss at that time was something of a tyrant. On my promotion he instructed me to organise an inventory for a toilet block which was constantly being vandalised by inebriated, fed-up, lonely, disgruntled, womanless airmen who wanted to take things out on something. Its usual condition was impaired by those who could not discriminate between a shower and a toilet pan. I also had to see that all necessary repairs were carried out. This duty entailed filling out the necessary documentation and liaising with the barrack warden, something not too easily done.

On entering my second year there, it was decided by the powers that be to change the length of time at Bahrain from two years to one year. That made me feel good – I think not! So many lads were suffering from L of S (lack of sex) and liver problems, from too much alcohol consumption, together with other ailments, and so many seemed to be going 'round the bend.'

Well, before my two years were up they changed it again to a nine-month posting. Did my morale a lot of good, I can tell you.

The opportunity arose from time to time, during my two years, 1960/62, at this luxury health resort (I jest), to act as the 'loadie' on the base Valletta aircraft. This aircraft frequently visited the nearby desert outposts where British servicemen were detached or were serving. The loads for these flights consisted mostly of fruit and vegetables together with other urgent supplies, and also the odd passenger.

This aircraft was not easy to work on whilst loading heavy freight. Two thirds of the weight had to be lifted forward of the spar, which stuck up about two feet across the inside of the fuselage and one third of the freight aft, evenly spread. If, for instance, you had a heavy load, you had to lift it over the spar, not an easy task in the confined space available. The aircraft didn't have a trim sheet, just one of those weight and balance forms.

This official document entailed gathering all the weights of the items loaded on the aircraft, including passenger weights, and working out the centre of gravity of the aircraft. There was much more, but I don't want to bore you. The chains and strainers supplied for securing the loads were also out of the Ark. Nets were not available to us then. The route took in both Sharjah and Muscat (Bait Al Falaj). At Sharjah there was an Air Movement Section, so that arrival/departure went off OK.

At Bait Al Falaj, the pilot, who incidentally was a sergeant, assisted by his navigator, a flying officer, had to circle around, looking out for any stray camels or goats, before landing on the stony surface. There were no buildings, air traffic control or airport staff at this desert airstrip.

I was privileged to occupy the Co-Pilot's seat on these trips. On one occasion when we landed at this airfield, there were two aircraft on the ground, an Avro York four-engine freighter and a single engine Scottish Pioneer utility aircraft.

We dropped off an army officer who was seconded to the Trucial Oman Scouts (TOS) and wore the Arab headdress of that regiment. He made his way over to the Pioneer, was greeted by the Army pilot and boarded the aircraft. The aircraft revved up, only going a few yards, and was airborne; it was blowing a bit, as the airstrip was on high ground.

When the loads off and on the Valetta were sorted, the sergeant pilot, the navigator and I wandered over to the York. Our pilot spoke to both the York's pilot and the 'flying spanner' (the flight engineer). They had brought in a heavy generator, which was being offloaded. I, being nosey, had a look in the aircraft.

What I saw made me gasp. There was no flooring whatsoever. Planks of wood were laid over the airframe cross members, to which the loads were tied with ropes. I nearly said secured… I cannot imagine that this aircraft would have passed any of the RAF's stringent airworthiness tests. Well, it probably did when it was in RAF colours.

On the way back, and throughout this flight, the skipper kept asking for coffee. This made me feel sick. I sort of ambled aft past the passengers, towards the loo. When I was inside, after making sure the door was shut, I coughed my heart up.

The aircraft landed whilst I was in there, bumped a bit and threw the contents of the Elsan toilet into my face. Just imagine the reception from the other passengers when I eventually plucked up courage to show my face.

Just to mention some of the privileges of living within the confines of the Camp. There was a NAAFI, which was run by the usual Indian immigrant workers. They made much effort to comply with the rules and serve the multitude of inebriated occupants.

At this time in history, airmen were not allowed to purchase bottles of spirits. It had only recently been authorized for spirits to be sold in the NAAFIs. They could only serve tots of shorts to airmen. Nevertheless, I, like others, got over this by ordering whatever took my fancy at the time. Some days it would be a pint of gin and lime, others it would be a pint of whisky and soda. All served in tots into a pint glass.

Tables and chairs were in short supply, especially the serviceable ones, so those fortunate enough to occupy them would take their chairs with them when ordering from the bar or when visiting the air conditioner outside. This air conditioner was surrounded by a sort of wicker fence, and at the entrance there was a crude sign saying 'BBC member's only' (BBC was Bahrain Bufty Club). This machine was used as target practice for those who sought danger by urinating as near as possible to the electrics of the thing. The smell was atrocious. This so-called club had one rule... be inside when it opened and when it was chucking-out time.

In my second year a 'Malcolm club' opened up, a similar establishment to the NAAFI. An English lady manageress, no less, came with it. This lady, who seemed to be well into her 60s, was so sought after that the men were like bees round a honeypot. By the number of notches etched on the outside of this building, it would seem that this brave lady comforted many a lonesome chappie.

In the Air Movements section we contracted for a large wooden, metal-lined cooler, supplied by the Coca Cola drinks company. This was frequently topped up with large chunks of ice and several different types of fizzy drinks. That was until the demand for payment got a bit excessive. It was placed on trust for each individual to put money into the pot, but somehow or other this didn't seem to be understood by many. It all sort of got forgotten when all the local labour got kicked off base after the Beverley was blown up.

Drinking all these soft fizzy drinks to try and satisfy our raging thirsts had terrible effects on our wind emissions. Would you believe we held competitions as to who could fart the longest and loudest, and one member of our esteemed group could actually control these eruptions to music. This was the most amusing sight to witness. There were also competitions to see who could explode talcum powder the furthest.

The airfield defence was carried out at different times by various regiments. I can recall the Inniskilling Fusiliers, the Coldstream Guards and the Paras; in turn they were billeted in the billet block next to ours. At times this caused great concern as they insisted on practising their procedures for loading and firing their mortar bombs in between the billets, using empty beer cans for this purpose.

All the shouting and ordering about caused much annoyance to those of us trying to rest after coming off night shift. This often resulted in an exchange of insults and blasphemy.

Naturally, we would get to know some of individuals within these regiments. The Inniskillings (Skins) were mostly short guys from Northern Ireland and always seemed to be fighting each other, usually after a bevy. I often had the privilege of writing letters for them to their mothers/fathers, wives, family members and sweethearts etc. I even, on occasions, read their letters to them, which could be quite embarrassing at times.

The Coldstream Guards were a different kettle of fish. They often told me stories of serving within London and the methods used for gaining extra cash. Put your hands over your eyes if you're squeamish.

They frequented various pubs in London, where those of a deviant mindset gathered to meet these very fit handsome soldiers. They told me that they were often asked, for large amounts of money, to undress for individuals or groups of men who would then proceed to pleasure themselves. Extra money could be earned for them to defecate or urinate in front of some of these individuals.

Even larger amounts of money could be earned for providing and performing sex with a lady in front of an audience. I was informed that there was no lack of willing lady participants. The Paras were, and I suppose are, an exceedingly tough collection of individuals.

I mentioned earlier about Beverley XM 110 being blown up. This aircraft was towed to the Paras compound and used by them as a training facility. You can view pictures of this aircraft on line.

The SNCOs and Warrant Officers of the Paras sometimes took over the duties of the RAF station Orderly Sergeant and Orderly Officer. This was noticeable in the NAAFI and Malcolm Club, especially at closing time, when they would come in, bang on a table and shout 'get out now!' The place used to empty straight away. Not like the attempts of the RAF Orderly Officers and the RAF Orderly Sgts.

They also stopped glasses being taken out of the premises. Prior to this everyone had taken filled glasses of booze into the billets. Their intervention in this procedure brought a temporary stop to all the broken glass that was constantly littering the place.

They also took responsibility for those confined within the guardroom, including RAF types. Witnessing these individuals alongside the main camp road segregating pebbles into different sizes was humiliating, even for those of us passing by. They also, purposely, made the prisoners double up and down camp roads, I suppose as a warning to anyone who thought of misbehaving. This punishment was carried out in the hottest part of the day, and the heat at times was unbearable.

One of our Duty Air Movements Officers (DAMO) was a

Warrant Officer. He also had responsibility of looking after the camp cinema, the Astra. When it was quiet at work, off he would go and do his bit at the cinema.

We would get our special 3-ton lift vehicle, which was called a scissors truck, load a couple of nice comfy chairs in the back, drive quietly up to the cinema wall, elevate the back of the vehicle and have a free show. Yes, he did know about it.

Across the water from Bahrain on the Saudi Arabian mainland, a short flight away, was a large American airbase called Dhahran. We used to listen to their music broadcasts. Well, sometimes we did. There were occasions when their automatic record changing machine got stuck and it would go on and on repeating itself, sometimes for hours. Of course on this American airbase, because it was in Saudi Arabia, no alcohol was allowed.

Once a week a Dakota DC3 would fly over and disgorge 30 or so American airmen who would be bent on consuming as large amounts of alcohol as they could in their short stay. Very often we would help in throwing them, totally incapacitated with drink, back on board their aircraft.

I had an incident with an American sailor one Christmas. Unknown to me he was drunk in our NAAFI, with his head in his arms on a table. I shook him to wish him a Happy Christmas, as everyone was shaking hands and wishing each other well. He stood up, looked at me, and knocked me out.

Several of the residents in our large block kept dogs, which at night were tied to their beds. At mealtimes the dog owners used to go around the mess hall asking for bones and other food suitable for their dogs. I remember one time a cook should have been on duty early one morning, but he was so drunk no one could wake him. His dog, a vicious thing, would not let anyone near him, so he was left alone. He of course got into trouble, and a new ruling about not keeping dogs in the billets came about as a result. He then got a hiding from some of the other dog owners.

I did get an official commendation whilst there; I was disappointed with the document itself. To me it didn't look grand enough!

For my 20th birthday, I received a present from my mum, a Parker fountain pen. It came in a lovely box. It was green and I was really thrilled to receive it.

A lot of time was spent writing letters, as it was the only method of communication with home and friends. Remember there was no access to telephones, no computers, only the Royal Mail. I even bought a new bottle of ink. I showed it to one of the lads I worked with, who thought it was brilliant and asked to borrow it. After a day or so I asked for it back. He kept making excuses, saying he hadn't finished writing yet. This went on until I flipped. I told him I wanted it right now.

He went off to his bed space and came back and put the pen on my bed. I unscrewed the top and the nib had been bashed flat. That was when I lost it and saw red, beating the living daylight out of him. He screamed like hell, and was covered in blood. I could have quite easily done some real damage to him if I hadn't been pulled off by several of the other lads in the billet. I was shaking with anger and wasn't going to let go of this. In the end he ordered a taxi, took me to the capital city, Manama, and bought me another pen. He was jealous. I did not let it stop there either.

Eventually my time in Bahrain was nearly up. My tour ex-date was the 2nd of September 1962, so in late August I waltzed down to Station headquarters to speak to a friendly clerk therein about my flight home to the UK. He quite casually informed me that I would have to wait another month for a Britannia aircraft flight, to see if a seat was available, as all the UK seats on the weekly Britannia had been allocated until that time. Being a lowly corporal, I was certainly not on the 'A' list priority of 'must go now'.

My mood zoomed to explosion point at this knowledge, but I was working on Air Movements and there was a Beverley. The crew informed me that they were departing on the 2nd of September via just about everywhere, hoping to eventually hit the UK. So I went back to SHQ and told the smarmy get that I had a seat on this Beverley. Would he please get authorization for me to exit this shite-hole and get back to Blighty? Well, bless him, he did!

Via everywhere was right. We stopped at Sharjah and Salalah, and then had two night stops at Khormaksar. Then onto Khartoum, then El Adem for another night's stop. Then continuing onto Nice and eventually the final destination, Abingdon –home at last.

I had been posted to my next station, which was RAF Benson, near Wallingford Berkshire. Yep! Onto an Air Movements section again. Boy did I feel lucky!

Now there's a tale or two to tell of my time at this base…

# CHAPTER 5

# RAF BENSON, 1962/65

I arrived at RAF Benson, near Wallingford, Berkshire, in the autumn of 1962 at the same time as the brand new Argosy Transport Squadrons were being formed, and joined one of the three Air Movements Shifts. I met up with some old buddies from RAF St. Mawgan.

I really lapped up my three years at this base; lovely countryside, great beer and all those nearby hospitals full of lovely nurses. I really got into 'first aid' there and enjoyed many a 'lesson' down on the banks of the River Thames.

It wasn't long before I was sent on a movements course at RAF Kidbrooke, in the London Borough of Greenwich. This detachment lasted six weeks, during which I and 29 others underwent training in all aspects of air, sea and land movement of personnel and freight. On completion of the course and passing the final exam I gained the trade annotation of Q-EQ-AM, which I think means Qualified Equipment and Air Movements. My trade now was 'Supplier 11, Q-EQ-AM.'

Kidbrooke started off as a gliding school in 1941, although the area these days is totally surrounded by housing. Over its operational life there were many different RAF units based there, including a Barrage Balloon Depot, No. 1 Stores Depot, a language school and an Air Publication and Forms store, to mention a few. There was some talk of 'Secret goings on' there as well over its lifetime. The Movements school was based there from 1954 until 1963 and my detachment was during November and December 1962 on No. 6 Junior Movements Course.

You never know what to expect when you are sent on a course, but this was some experience. I remember that for me the course was easy, as I had just completed two years on Air Movements work in Bahrain. By that I mean it wasn't stressful. The instructors were authoritative and accommodating. The curriculum included both surface and air movements, with little problems thrown in for good measure, which included planning a road or barge route with a large load and several obstacles which you had to avoid, like low bridges, roadworks etc. Shipping, canal, rail and air movements were also taught.

With the West End of London on our doorstep it was fantastic. In addition, the Dover Patrol pub was only a stone's throw away down the road. We seemed to have lots of sessions in there during the six weeks of the course. The pub was easily identifiable by its sign, a ship in choppy waters in the English Channel. It has long since been pulled down and the area is now a housing estate.

There was of course a rush to get to the West End on the tube after ceasing work each day and to get the forces free tickets for all the big shows. These were obtainable from the Union Jack Club (A sort of serviceman's/women's hotel) which always seemed to be full of Wrens (Women's Royal Naval Service). Watching them dance in formation was something to behold.

One or two of the course members also took advantage of the many other forms of entertainment that were on offer in our capital city. Some, it seemed, never got out of Soho.

It was quite a treat to watch some of the lads first thing in the mornings running from the Tube station and trying to make it in time for the first lesson, having stayed out all night, missing a night's kip and the excellent food that was on offer. All the meals were first rate.

I even took advantage of the RAF Dental Services, whose London clinic at that time was in Harley Street; I made several visits to have my front teeth capped.

There was no airfield at Kidbrooke, although we did have a Hastings aircraft fuselage, minus the wings, to practise loading/unloading on. The Flight Sergeant (Chiefy) Instructor used the cockpit for growing tomatoes in, which was out of bounds to us 'erks.'

My Kidbrooke experience was something special; it was memorable for all the right reasons. All of us were young and looking for adventure. The time spent there, because of its location in London, was second to none. It was an eye opener and a learning curve in itself. There is now a school, the Thomas Tallis School, occupying the site.

On returning to Benson I bought a car, a TR1 Triumph Roadster. Wow, did I like this machine! But I eventually got rid of it when a long detachment came up. I paid £120 for it and sold it to another air mover for £50. Anyway it leaked oil from the engine rocker box.

I took my driving test in this vehicle, at Henley-on-Thames. It took two goes to pass. The first time, I met the examiner and we both walked to the car park, some 200 yards or so. We got into the car. He told me to start up and drive out of the car park, turning right. Well, I had just got to the exit, or so I thought, when he hit the dashboard with his clip-board, saying, 'Mr Davis, shall we start the test properly by not leaving the car park by the No Exit sign?' Yep, he failed me! I took it some weeks later and passed, much to my delight.

I used to go off to Wallingford for a night of liquid refreshment in my favourite drinking hole and general entertainment, and one of these occasions really miffed me. I parked up in a car park, which incidentally had no lighting, and spent the evening, as you do, talking utter tosh to all the region's beauties, excelling in my prowess on the dartboard and thoroughly enjoying sinking copious amounts of Watney's Red Barrel. When I staggered back to my chariot in the said parking lot, the bloody thing would not start. On close inspection I happened to notice that some person or persons unknown had nicked my battery. I had a long walk back to camp, via a visit to the local PC Plod, who was wearing his bicycle clips. He took notes and said he would keep a lookout. I was impressed!

I woke up a couple of moaning fellow 'blue jobs,' who were not best pleased at being withdrawn from their fantasies at that hour of the day, at 0200 hours, and borrowed a car battery, and one of the lads drove me to Wallingford to retrieve my treasured 'pash wagon'.

The summertime's spent here were wonderful; this part of our great country is beautiful in springtime and throughout the summer. With the Thames running through Wallingford and all the boats and festivals to attend, it was a young man's dream of a posting.

The winters when I was there, were, as a contrast, horrible. On my return to Benson in December 1962, the weather turned really bad. The snow on the airfield in places was over six feet deep. It had completely closed the runway. Our section building was even worse, as the snow had drifted against the building, as high as the one-storey roof. We had to dig our way in through the double doors, making an eight-foot-wide slippery channel to gain entrance. I had joined one of the three shifts, on a 24 hours on and 48 hours off duty roster.

So there we were having a nice cup of tea and playing cards, and it was freezing outside, which was putting a stop to our usual loading/unloading of the Argosys, when all of a sudden there was an almighty crash against the section main entrance doors. Everyone rushed out to find the Station Commander (A Group Captain) trying to extricate himself from his Land Rover. One of the double doors was bedded into the front bumper of his vehicle. He did not seem best pleased, and demanded to know where the Senior Air Movements Officer (SAMO) was. The Station Commander incidentally gave the impression that he was a tadge angry – OK, he was livid. He forced his way through our attempt to rescue him, shouting out the SAMO's surname and racing his way along the corridor at the speed of light into his office, whereupon a loud 'friendly chat' erupted at the highest noise decimal reading known to man. It was a one-way conversation. It seemed that the Station Commander wanted to know why the SAMO's manpower was not on the runway, like all the other staff, helping to clear the snow and ice away. This shouting carried on outside our crew room door as the CO was making his way out of the building. Incidentally, as he reversed off in his Land Rover he took one side of the entrance door with him, until it dislodged itself some metres away.

Well, all of a sudden we were issued with shovels and bass brooms, the three shifts, changed to eight hours and everyone on the runway throughout the 24-hour period was clearing away snow and ice. Even the WRAFs had been press-ganged into dishing out tea and wads on that ice cold runway. Most of the time not much was achieved, as it was constantly blowing a gale with sleet and snow.

Then to our surprise six large flame-emitting road tar burners turned up. Our job was to shift as much snow out of the way as possible so that these vehicles could line up in formation along the width of the runway. They blasted away blowing flames from beneath them like a collection of dragons. What they achieved was to melt the ice on the runway, which then proceeded to freeze again at the edge, creating an ice mound either side of the runway.

We were provided with some entertainment for a while in the daytime by the nearby RAF station at Abingdon, who kindly sent over several of their large Beverley aircraft, dropping bales of straw, to further cause embarrassment to our senior officers.

When sufficient runway clearance was obtained, two of our Argosy aircraft were dispatched to RAF Odiham, empty except for essential equipment. My shift partners and I went via road convoy to this base to meet up with the aircraft. We took all the necessary role equipment for the aircraft, together with tents and other camping equipment, including a field kitchen and the cooks.

It transpired that after loading all this equipment onto the two aircraft, leaving room and seating for ourselves, and of course the cooks, we took off for, of all places, Scotland! It was one of those 'Need to know' detachments. In other words, we did not know where we were going or for how long. We already had our cold wet weather gear on due to the low temperatures we were experiencing; little did we know how important that was. We landed at a desolate Scottish airfield, which we found out was called Milltown. It was an abandoned Royal Naval Fleet Air Arm airfield, previously called RNAS Fulmar 11, just south east of Lossiemouth on the Moray Firth.

Hang on a minute – there were no buildings there, save a hangar that was full of caravans, owned by Royal Navy personnel who were at sea. So guess who had to erect all the tents and marquees?

Two aircraft were sent there, as there was not enough aircraft parking space available for any more. Fortunately there was no snow on the ground, although we were soon to be affected by the wind chill factor, the rain and the openness of the place. The aircraft operated the normal schedules, as if they were back at base. Because we did not have the necessary loading vehicles, ie forklifts and Bedford three tonners, all the loads had to be loose loaded. There were no pallets or side guidance loads.

Working on the aircraft with tight turnaround times was doubly difficult, with freezing hands, and using the chains and strainers to secure the loads was painful and threatened frostbite.

The flying took place throughout the daylight hours – our two aircraft flew off and two more would arrive, and so on. There was no airfield lighting available, and even the refuelling vehicles had to be brought in. The airfield had been derelict for quite a few years. We thought we had it bad until we saw what the poor old cooks had to contend with, in handling their field kitchens.

The abandoned airfield at Milltown, formerly RNAS Fulmar 11, was originally built as a 'decoy' for RNAS Fulmar 1 (Lossiemouth) just to the North West.

Messing with those Tilley lamps for warmth and light in the tents almost became a full-time occupation. Two things we learnt quickly were not to touch the lamp wicks the mantle and of course try not to touch the insides of the tents. If you did it would cause drips of water that could soak our kit, which soon got into a poor condition.

There were no showers available, just as well as no one felt like getting undressed. Using the temporary tented ablutions was a scary experience too. When you had to go, it was very cold about the nether regions.

This was a two-week affair, the longest time to date that I had gone without a proper wash or shave.

It became dark quite early. After work, apart from trying to get some warm grub inside us, there was literally nothing to do. I discovered that the local town of Elgin was about three or four miles away. As we didn't have any transport, I suggested that I would lead an expedition on foot to discover the delights of the local alehouses. So off we went in the pitch blackness. We arrived at the location of the first hostelry we found at about 2130 hours, tired, very thirsty and somewhat weary from our enforced march.

Hang on a minute - the place was shut, no lights on, all was locked up! After banging on doors, shouting and emitting general expressions of displeasure, an upstairs window was opened slightly and a foreign-sounding gentleman said to us in a somewhat loud voice, 'The pubs here close at 9 pm, so piss off you Sassenachs!'

No one had told us that the pubs in Scotland shut at 2100. After informing the whole community of our displeasure, we trudged the whole way back to our tented camp singing at the top of our voices - sober.

Eventually we returned to RAF Benson. On reporting for duty I was informed that a billet inspection was to be carried out, so geeing up the blokes up for that was quite challenging. Also I had been selected for Orderly Corporal, and to top it off, I had to report for Ground Defence Training (GDT). This was an annual requirement which had to be completed before leave passes could be authorized. You had to have a session on the rifle range, receive lectures on what to do if a nuclear explosion took place, wear gas masks and loads of other stuff. The lectures were carried out by an

RAF Regiment Flight Sergeant, who informed the assembled gathering that on promotion to that rank he was not issued with feathers, he was not a Red Indian and would not tolerate being called 'Chiefy'. It was assumed by all those present that his demand for respect, whilst showing none for any of us, was as a result of still suffering from the after effects of the operation which all those of a similar position in the RAF Regiment had to undergo – ie, his brain had been removed and concrete inserted in its place.

I was also pleased to see that the section main entrance door had been repaired.

A loading team on Air Movements consisted of six people, a corporal and five airmen. There was also a sergeant and an officer. When I got back from my Scottish expedition, I was surprised to find that we had another member of the team. A corporal, this individual had been a warrant officer signaller throughout the war. He had rejoined the RAF and been given the rank of corporal. He was supposed to be with me to learn the ropes, so to speak, but all he was interested in was getting as much alcohol down his throat as his pittance of pay would allow, and if he could cadge money off any unsuspecting idiot who lent him any. They would of course never see it again!

On arrival he found that one of our officers had been on his squadron during the war, so they became good buddies. He was for me a liability, not interested in doing anything; his head was too far up his own arse, and he lived for what he used to be during the war. He often boasted about his six kids, but never of going to see them. All he did was swan around showing off his signaller's brevet and his chest full of medals. I came across many like him in the RAF.

No wonder that the Argosys did not have a very long life in the RAF (74 built, 56 in use by the RAF). Their payload for short distances was great, say between Benson and Wildenrath in Germany, but any further and the offered payload was abysmal. Nevertheless, at Benson, there was a lot to do and the Argosys kept us movers busy with regular schedules and all sorts of odd-shaped loads to contend with, and of course special operations.

I can't remember how often, but every now and then we had to do a special procedure. Hidden in the back of the cargo shed we had a coffin-shaped box and some other associated equipment, all painted matt black and kept under a large tarpaulin. An aircraft would arrive specially for us to handle this equipment; sometimes it was a Britannia, other times a VC10 and on occasion one of our own Argosys. We would then have to practise loading and unloading a coffin, dressed in white overalls, onto a freshly painted lorry, specially draped for the practice. The lorry then proceeded to the newly-built Church of England church on the camp. Each time there was lots of top brass watching and making notes. Speculation was rife as to why this was being done. We eventually guessed the answer, and later it was proved right. It was practice for the bringing home of the Duke of Windsor. He eventually died on 28th May 1972 at his home in Paris and was brought back to England via RAF Benson.

I spent a year in the cargo shed dealing with imports and exports of military equipment, often travelling to the railway station at Wallingford to dispatch or collect air freight. The reason I was sent to be in charge of the Cargo Shed was because I had fallen out with my shift sergeant. He was another ex-aircrew navigator bod, who had left the RAF and come back in as a sergeant.

We worked 24-hour shifts, 24 on 48 off. During stand-downs we were supposed to be readily available, just in case anything turned up, and I used to bog off down town. I know it's a bit naughty!

So I got back to camp, after a meeting with my future wife, when I was confronted by one of the lads, who informed me that a lorry had arrived during the evening that required offloading with a fork-lift. So as yours truly was unavailable this shift sergeant, the only other chap on our shift who had a F1629 RAF driving licence, got called out from his married quarter. It would appear that he was a tadge upset at this and wanted me up before the Squadron Leader. The next day, the Sqn/Ldr and I had a lovely chat, honest. He was a lovely fellow (kept calling me 'Davy Boy'). I got a bit miffed myself with this sergeant chappie and handed in my F1629. I thought, that'll teach the bastard, he'll have to do all the driving from now on. After a bit he was insisting that Motor Transport section be called for each time, but that didn't always work as MT did not always have a driver available. I used to watch him drive the forks, which infuriated him to the extreme.

My year in the cargo shed finished when a further detachment of one month's duration came about to RAF El Adem near Tobruk in Libya. Yes, that was tented accommodation as well. The weather was very hot and humid throughout the day and near freezing cold at night. I was to visit this airfield an awful lot later on in my career.

I was to be sent on many more detachments from Benson, some of short duration, flying into air shows for instance when we carried out demonstrations of quickly loading and unloading vehicles, from landing to taking off, with vehicles off and others loaded on within 20 minutes.

Another trip that springs to mind was to Denmark, where there was lots of snow about but at least we had warm, decent accommodation. The working arrangements on the airfield were carried out within a collection of large marques and tents. This was the last occasion when I actually got involved in an exchange of knuckles with someone. I broke my silver signet ring in the process. The punch up-was with another former Boy Entrant like me from the 29th entry suppliers. He got relegated to the 30th entry for failing the finals; he failed the second try as well. He took over my girlfriend when I left Cosford, made her pregnant, married her and after a short while she dumped him. He never got over the fact that she fancied me more than him. I cannot remember the exchange of words, but there was a lot of blood and snot (all his) about the place.

This detachment over, I returned to base and again went on shift, I took out my RAF driving licence again. We had a lovely officer (Polish wartime pilot) as our Duty Air Movements Officer (DAMO). He walked a bit lopsided, I gathered because of all the medals on his left chest. His spoken English was not all that good, but he was a lovely chap.

Having got rid of my Triumph, I bought a clapped-out Hillman Minx. I went to a petrol station one time to buy a half crown's worth of fuel. I kept the engine running as it was difficult to start, and I could not get back into the car, as the door was stuck! I eventually got in after a load of kicking and pulling of the door. It took about 15 minutes messing about trying to open the thing. This car kept stopping because the carburettor kept filling up with rust sludge from the petrol tank. Every few miles I had to take the carb off and clean it out, even when I was courting Lita.

Another time, after taking a load of lads to a Wallingford hostelry for a lunchtime session, we were on the way back when I stopped at a road junction. When it was clear I let out the clutch, moved forward a couple of yards and the rear left wheel fell off. So scratching around for another cheap heap on wheels took place. I bought a Ford V8 Pilot for fifty quid. I needed these wheels, as I was heavily into courting my girlfriend Lita at this time. I had this vehicle for some time before the gearbox disintegrated into a pile of mashed metal.

I used to get stopped a lot by the police driving this car. After one particularly unpleasant incident with two over-officious 'woodentops' I wrote to the Chief Constable to complain about it, and they sent a Chief Inspector to interview me. I had to laugh when he arrived at the camp. I spoke to him on the phone and arranged to meet him, as he was unfamiliar with the way the camp road system was arranged. I waved at him and watched him drive down a 'No Entry' road. He wasn't too pleased when I pointed it out to him. Incidentally nothing came of my complaint, as I had no independent witnesses.

It was now 1965, and I received notification that I was posted to Germany, though no station was mentioned. This was later changed to Cyprus, where I was to join the newly formed Near East Air Force (NEAF) Mobile Air Movements Section (MAMS) at RAF Akrotiri.

I got married to Lita on the 29th March 1965 in Wallingford. My best man was another corporal who had been allocated to me to learn the ropes. On his previous posting he had been a flight sergeant, and he had arrived at Benson via the military prison at Colchester. Lita and I as newly-weds lived for a short while at a village called Cholsey, in a rented ground floor flat about two miles outside Wallingford. It was near to where she was nursing, in a hospital called 'Fair Mile.' Actually it was a nut house.

The main railway line from London to Bristol was at the rear of the property, and we joined along with hundreds of others to watch the train carrying Sir Winston Churchill's funeral corsage pass through. We might as well have not bothered, as the train ripped though at about 90 miles an hour.

Now carless, I signed out an RAF bicycle and got quite fit cycling to and from Benson on shift about six miles each way. This lasted for just over a month, before I was off to pastures new in Cyprus.

My dad, 1928

Dad in 1953

School group, me on the teacher's left

At RAF St Mawgan, 1959

RAF Bahrain

Bahrain

In Bahrain with Charlie Chester

RAF Benson

At RAF Benson

RAF Al Adem

El Adem

NEAF MAMS, 1966 - oil lift

Condec loading vehicle

Meeting a VIP - a Russian Admiral

Greeting Dana and her daughter

Day out for a brave young man

Award ceremony

Greeting the Squadron Padre

Boy Entrant insignia, RAF Cosford 1956/58

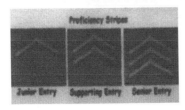

Proficiency Stripes

Junior Entry    Supporting Entry    Senior Entry

My uniforms – Bristol Airport

Duty Crew     Airport     Assistant Terminal     Terminal Duty
Duty Officer     Manager     Manager

My hat badge

After a regrading I reverted to a blazer and flannels, eventually
wearing double-breasted suits

CHAPTER 6

# RAF AKROTIRI, 1965-68

## NEAR EAST AIR FORCE MOBILE
## AIR MOVEMENTS (NEAFMAMS)

I had previously volunteered myself for duties on Mobile Air Movements, expecting to be posted onto one of the teams at RAF Abingdon, where the United Kingdome MAMS (UKMAMS) teams had their UK base. Mobile Air Movements Teams are responsible for turning around RAF aircraft at non-RAF bases, as well as other special missions.

On arrival at RAF Akrotiri, after all the necessary arrival paperwork had been completed, it was confirmed by the Senior Air Movements Officer that I was joining the newly-formed Near East Air Force Mobile Air Movements (NEAFMAMS) section. Indeed I was the first one to arrive; no one else had as yet turned up.

I found that our accommodation was a Tyneham hut behind the Air Movements Section. It took about two weeks for all the twelve of us to gather together. We were split into two teams, each consisting of an officer, a flight sergeant, a sergeant, a corporal and two airmen.

I learnt that the unit was designated on the RAFs 'Special Duty List' of personnel, which, as far as I could make out only entitled us to avoid being selected for station duties. In the meantime, while everyone was assembling to join our newly-formed section, the sergeant, personal assistant (PA) to the rather toffee-nosed speaking senior air movement's officer, (SAMO) wanted me as his personal 'fag.' He kept calling for me to do his bidding to collect tea and buns, etc. from the NAAFI wagon. That, I might add, really got up my nose.

We started off with helping out the Air Movements Section to turn around some of their aircraft, much to the delight of the lads on this section, who honed up their catcalling skills towards us in the process.

The very first base job we did as a team was nothing to do with aircraft. It was on a ship, anchored outside the Cypriot three-mile limit. We had to offload thousands of individually boxed missiles, each about eight feet long. I drove our new tractor forklift on board and into the hold, loading the missiles onto nets to be winched up and transferred onto Army Pontoon boats for ferrying to shore. This took about four days to complete.

It was interesting to speak to the crew members and listen to their moans, although they did mention that because the ship's load was 'explosives' they received extra pay.

We managed to get a sort of system together for offloading these missiles onto the three army pontoons, which when loaded up, then sped off to shore for storage in the bomb stores. There were only three of us doing the work.

I was driving our new tractor fork-lift, a Massey Fergusson T21 tractor with a double fork attachment at the front and a large balance box at the rear. This could be filled with either water or sand. While we were loading the first batch of missiles onto the netting for craning to the top deck, a hooter sounded, which turned out to be the ship's cook informing us that tea was ready. So everyone except me disappeared to the top deck for a bun and a cuppa. Silly me, I thought I would load a couple of these nets to save a bit of time, as I was enjoying myself doing so, so I decided to wait and go for tea after the others returned.

So after the others got back I climbed up to the top deck for some tea; I found out where the mess was and entered. I spoke to what looked like the ship's cook and asked him about having a cup of tea, and something to eat. He said, in his best matelot's voice, 'You can piss off matey, teatime is over.' And that was it for me, no tea or eats.

I had to live in in the airmen's quarters during the three months waiting for my wife to join me, and we had only been married for three months. On one of these days I took my dhobi (laundry) to the camp laundry, on arrival, and I was astounded to see that the Indian gent in charge was the same person who had the laundry set-up in Bahrain.

During these first months of operation, we as a team started to get familiar with some of the destinations in different Middle East countries which would, in the next three years, become like second homes to us. During this initial stage of settling in our new section, one of the two flight sergeants seemed to stand out somewhat; he originated from the Emerald Isle. It became noticeable that when we went on detachments, he never came with us, so I asked him why. He said he was the section admin officer and looked after things when we were gone. This seemed acceptable - that was until the wives came out to join us. Much later at Nicosia I queried this with him, as no attempt by him or anyone else had been made to keep our wives up to date or deliver money or the much-needed post. He said he didn't have a driving licence. I thought this setup was rather odd, as he was supposed to be part of a team, although it would seem he thought differently.

He also stood out in that he wore a khaki drill (KD) uniform different from everyone else's. Everyone had to wear the authorized KD, which was shorts, short-sleeve shirts, beret and khaki socks up to the knee. He wore tailored clothing, consisting of long trousers, long-sleeved shirt and black tie and his peaked hat, the sort of uniform bought in Singapore from civilian tailors.

It was also noticeable that he kept disappearing onto the aircraft parking area (the pan). I found he was seeing every transport aircraft 'off chocks', and as it taxied away to the runway, he would stand to attention and salute it until it left the area.

I could see that our CO, by his expression, was getting comments from fellow officers, as we undoubtedly were from fellow airmen on other sections, who witnessed these strange events with hilarity. I'll come onto the outcome of the relationship with him and our CO later on.

Lita, like all the wives, had to undergo a three-month separation before being allowed overseas. This was to allow the men time to acclimatize and to give those like me time to look for rented accommodation. I opted for a brand new first-floor flat, which was next to a dried-up river bed, alongside a roadway. Lita arrived on a Friday and I was granted a fortnight's leave.

The following Friday, there was a knock on the door of our new-found flat. I answered, to be told by a fellow on my team that the whole unit was being posted to Nicosia. We had to report for duty at Nicosia on Monday morning. Nicosia, by the way, was in the region of 70 miles away.

So this other married airman and I (incidentally for quite a number of years we remained in contact with each other) ordered a taxi to take both us and our wives the 70-odd miles to Nicosia, once again, to search for somewhere to live, only this time Lita had a say in it. The fare for the taxi was paid for by the new landlord in Nicosia. After looking at several houses offered for rent we chose a bungalow within a large fenced-off garden with an open-sided garage in the district of Nicosia, which was authorized for servicemen to live in. It was called Ayios Dhometrios.

The other lad and his wife opted for a bungalow which was near ours, the only difference being that his new landlord had built a shed at the bottom of his garden for him, his wife and kids to live in.

Then we had to go back to Akrotiri to arrange transport and the associated paperwork – and remember, it was over a weekend. The transport offered to us for the move to Nicosia was a three-ton lorry, which was not all that comfortable for the ladies. The officers and the SNCOs were provided with cars. Gosh. it's a wonderful experience being at the bottom of the pile.

During our short stay in Limassol before leaving this flat, Lita called me to have a look out of the window one morning. We had previously seen, just up the road from us, a Greek Cypriot family living at the side of the road in a shack the size of a garden shed made from bits of tin and wood. In this shack lived a pregnant woman, a child, and presumably her husband. Next to this was a telegraph pole with a water pipe rising up about four feet, with a tap at its top. There was also a broken piece of mirror nailed onto the pole. This one morning the lady had obviously had the baby and was washing it and herself under the tap, and all that traffic passing close by.

Then we were off to our new station, RAF Nicosia. These were the early days of the NEAF Mobile Air Movements, and the manpower was organized so that two SNCOs would do all the supervision, especially when we had soldiers or locals to do the physical work. This only happened once, on the Oil Lift in Nairobi. It was essential and obvious that everyone should be able to drive. Out of the original twelve of us I was the only airman with a driving licence who took out a F1629 (RAF driving permit).

Would you believe it, further to upset us all the SNCOs had just completed a movements course before being posted to Cyprus. What an absolute shambles, with no previous experience on working on aircraft.

## RAF Nicosia, 1965

So we started another round of filling in forms designed to let each RAF section know that we had arrived. I had no transport of my own to get to work, but managed to get a lift with my other team member, who had bought a motorbike.

We then had to get familiar with the layout of RAF Nicosia, which incidentally covered a large area. Our section accommodation was a large hut close to the Air Movements section, which incidentally were smaller premises. We introduced ourselves to the station air movement's section, which consisted of a sergeant, a corporal and a senior aircraftsman (SAC). They were a good bunch of chaps who were struggling to cope with the air movement's traffic. This, no doubt, was one of the reasons why we were posted to this airfield.

Nicosia was also a civilian airport, with scheduled services to destinations far and wide. The RAF was involved in the training of the local people with aircraft refuelling, fire and rescue and Air Traffic Control amongst other things.

RAF Nicosia was in the process of closing down. Our section was sent there for any diversion aircraft not being able to land at Akrotiri for some reason or other.

The corporal air mover on the station Air Movements section was a lovely chap called Smudge. He loved playing cricket and was a dab hand at producing curries. I used to exchange Christmas cards with him for many years, before his final posting came through for entry to the pearly gates. I bet he cadged his way in.

Dear old Smudge had his girlfriend flown out, at his own expense of course. She was already married, and this meant he was not entitled to any overseas allowances. This resulted in him having one or two spending power difficulties, and he was always skint.

For some unknown reason he befriended an RAF policeman and lodged in the spare room of his private accommodation. Smudge was not allowed, officially, to live out of the camp gates either. He got himself into serious debt and owed money to, I suspect, half the RAF people in Cyprus.

About a year later when I was at Akrotiri I met him in the air cargo shed, as he had brought his personal effects down for flying home to the UK. As he was helping to offload them from a lorry, a group of RAF policemen appeared and took over the task, opening all his boxes. I never did find out the explanation for this.

One of the regular visitors to Nicosia airport was an El Al Britannia aircraft, whose crew watched over all the work being carried on or around their aircraft; it wasn't long before they requested our assistance in providing these facilities, each time they flew in.

During the four initial months at Nicosia we settled into working on the 70 Squadron Hastings aircraft that were in residence. They operated a regular weekly service to RAF El Aden, in Libya, with passengers and freight, also a weekly service with fruit and vegetables, and sometimes the loads were frozen animal carcasses. We had to go with them to unload. During one of these loading episodes, just as we had completed loading, several tons of carcasses were thawing and dripping blood. We were informed by the 'friendly' 70 Squadron engineering personnel that the aircraft was unserviceable and wouldn't be going anywhere. So we had to quickly offload all the meat back onto a refrigerated lorry.

We were now dressed for flying in long-sleeved KD shirts with black ties and long KD trousers. As we were not going anywhere, our flying officer boss told me to go to MT to collect our Land Rover and bring it back to collect the rest of the team.

Off I went, walking over a mile in the scorching heat to the MT compound to collect the vehicle. On arrival, I presented myself at the sliding glass window of the MT Section office. There were two people inside, an airman and a sergeant. As I asked to book out the MAMS Land Rover, the Motor Transport (MT) sergeant made an appearance and asked for my F1250 identity card. He then promptly charged me for being improperly dressed. He would not listen to any explanation, as any normal person with half a brain would have done.

I drove the Land Rover back to collect the others, totally perplexed. I explained the situation to our flying officer boss, who kindly got on the phone and spoke to the sergeant, who then grudgingly dropped the charge.

I bet you're thinking that there was a lot more to it than the above explanation. Yep – you're right.

Our CO at that time was a Flight Lieutenant, a Scot and a strict disciplinarian. It was very difficult trying to conform to his demands as he was the sort of officer who would not listen to any suggestions or advice, especially from subordinates.

We were now experiencing the delights of flying around to several other countries, with 70 Squadron, which included Libya Turkey and Iran.

One of my pals, a nearby resident in Nicosia, recounted an incident near his house in Ayios Dimitrios when there was a raging gun battle taking place, which left a dead Turk lying in the road for several days in the heat. He had to get past the body to get to work when all had died down. His wife was pregnant at the time.

This incident is referred to in one of Dawn French's books. Her father was an RAF sergeant, who, incidentally, later committed suicide.

Living in the bungalow we had interesting neighbours. On one side were two randy American sailors, on the other a minister of the Cypriot government. He had an Egyptian lady living with him, who he referred to as his wife. Oh yeah? He was about 60 years old. One time he had to go to Geneva for a conference, and he even shipped his big American car over there to use. While he was away his lady friend took a fancy to a young Greek Cypriot policeman. On his return all the local gossips could not wait to tell him of this liaison. He then ejected her quite unceremoniously, quite loudly too. She had obviously broken her contract with him.

A bit later I invited him in for coffee and a chat – we often had these meetings. I asked him where his wife was, as we had not seen her lately. Mind you the only time we seemed to see her was when she hung out her knickers to dry. We already knew where she was, as we had seen her down in the city with her new chap. He said that her parents in Egypt were ill and she had returned home to look after them. Yeah right! Well, he was a politician.

I bought a dog, a Labrador pup, a lovely animal. We named him Kim. He kept Lita looked after whilst I was constantly away. At the bungalow garden entrance, we had a very old grapevine, arranged in an arch over the gateway. That was until Kim chewed his way through it. Saying our Greek landlord was upset would really be missing the point – he was furious. Even trying to bribe him with a bottle of malt and a crate of Tennents' didn't help smooth things out. He suggested, 'You kill dog, Mr Gerry!'

I bought a new car; it was a small Mazda hatchback, a lovely car too. Cost me £465. We saw them on display in the showroom and decided to buy one to ease the transport situation when I was back at base. This decision arose as a result of arriving five minutes late for work one day. I was a pillion passenger on one of the lads' motorbikes. The CO told me in no uncertain manner that I and the other lad were both late and not to let it happen again or there would be consequences. The bus we should both have been on suddenly appeared at the base of the camp road, so I could not help mentioning to the CO that if we had caught the official means of transport we would have been even later – in actual fact we were early!

He saw red, took me to one side and threatened me with an insubordination charge. He also said that the bus being late was of no consequence, as it was our responsibility to be on time for work. Incidentally there was nothing to do other than sit around and do his bidding. I might only have been a lowly corporal, but I saw red too. I suggested that I was not being insubordinate or disrespectful, merely pointing out the situation as I saw it. I also might have mentioned that I thought I was being unnecessarily bullied by him. I thought he was going to burst with rage – he certainly looked like it. He was in my opinion totally devoid of common sense.

Many years later I discovered that he had become a vicar.

Back to the process of buying the car. The car salesman told Lita and me that we could not have one of the display models; we had to go to Famagusta, which was about 35 miles away, to collect one from the docks.

He took us both there in an air-conditioned American car. We got there and there was a bit of a kerfuffle in gaining entrance to the dockside warehouse where the imported cars were kept. To our surprise therein lay about 30 new cars all neatly lined up, most of them riddled with bullet holes. There was a lovely blue one tucked away in a far-off corner, and Lita liked the colour, so we chose that one.

We were both dubious about going along this road as we were aware that very often there was an exchange of shooting and following that, many atrocities ensued as a result. On the way there we passed a large village, the site of many battles and terrible goings on, which was totally abandoned. All the windows and doors had been spirited away, nicked, in other words. Quite a picture to behold!

Lita wanted to buy a sewing machine, to help her keep busy when I was away. We went to the NAAFI shop and she selected one, but it was too dear, about £60, and I couldn't afford it. The manager said 'what are you quibbling about? Get it on the never-never'. this worried me sick. It was only over three months, but it was the first time we had ventured into an HP agreement. As a result of owning this machine she developed several friendships through making and altering ladies' clothing.

## NEAF MAMS Nairobi, 1966

Christmas 1965 just about over, we suddenly got tasked to go back to Akrotiri. It was unclear why we had to do this, although it was probably known by our bosses. But it soon became clear, as the news of the independence declaration by Ian Smith in Rhodesia was world headline news.

We soon found ourselves in Nairobi, Kenya; the shock was that we had to stay there for three months. It became known as the 'Oil Lift'.

So there was Lita and five other wives stranded in Nicosia, not knowing each other, having just recently arrived from the UK via a short stopover in Akrotiri. Within this short space of time they all had to seek two different houses in two different foreign towns, abandoned and with no one to give them any form of assistance. We could hardly go home for the weekend, could we? At that time we did not have a TV, radio or phone. Even mail was a problem, as there was no one to collect it and deliver it to the wives. I nearly had a fit with my boss over this. Also the wives had to get a taxi to the camp and go through an embarrassing procedure to get any money. The only people who had bank accounts in those days were the officers.

I decided to write to Lita from Nairobi, via the ordinary mail and not the British Forces Postal Office (BFPO) service. It was costing me one shilling and threepence a day to post a letter. A lot of money in those days – well it was for me!

When the Oil Lift first got under way in December 1965, UKMAMS operated from an airfield in Dar-es-Salaam in Tanzania, but this caused huge diplomatic upheavals, so we were all dispatched to the civil airport at Nairobi, called at that time Embakasi (it is now called Jomo Kenyatta International Airport). There were other teams sent to Lusaka and Endola.

When we arrived, early in January 1966, we were at first accommodated in the Kenyan Air Force (KAF) billets at RAF Eastleigh, until they wanted their billets back, as they were initiating a large recruitment dive. So from then onwards we dossed down at the Spread Eagle Hotel on the outskirts of Nairobi. What a place! All the rooms were on the ground floor. The rooms were small, with two beds to a room. Wow, we even had a balcony! So I opened the balcony door and saw that someone had kindly left a washing line hanging outside on this balcony. For some reason I leant on this line and one of our widows sprang open. So a bit of engineering on my part took place.

Throughout both of my three-month detachments at this place, there was a lot of thieving by the Africans.

At work we had six RAF Britannia aircraft to play with. At least we did eventually – at first all sorts of civilian charter aircraft were commandeered to assist with the job we were there to do. This was to ferry aviation gasoline to the Zambian airfields of Lusaka and Endola. The fuel was in 44-gallon drums, and 56 of these were loaded into each aircraft, which was then chained down to the aircraft floor. A lot of heavy work, I can tell you.

The Javelin jet fighters from our base in Cyprus were also dispatched to the Zambian airfields as fighter protection. Before they left they all had to be painted, as they were near the end of their flying lives and no two looked the same.

We had 12 African helpers allocated to two 12-hour shifts to help with all the physical work; most of them were excellent workers, although one or two did get the chop for various reasons, mostly for not turning up for work. They got paid fortnightly and after getting their hands on the dosh they promptly spent it on booze or paying off loans and were skint the next day - their ladies never saw any of it.

I remember one of the African workers telling me that his woman was sick. As I had a packet of aspirins in my 'nav bag' where I kept all the paperwork, I gave them to him. The look on his face was amazing, he was really grateful; mind you I don't know if he ever gave them to her!

The whole detachment of us Air Movers and the Techs upset the newly-appointed Kenyan chief airport security officer. He objected to our apparel, in that we were mostly scruffy as hell and didn't take any notice of him when he came strutting around.

Amongst other things he did not like us eating dressed like this in the airport terminal restaurant or hanging around the arrivals hall ogling all the hostesses and female passengers. As a result of his intervention we had to dine in a cordoned-off area of the staff eating place (oops, I nearly called it a restaurant).

There was an attempt at using another form of fuel container on the Britannias; it was a large round rubber ball with a capacity of around 400 gallons with 'D' rings at both sides. After a short trial they were abandoned, as they kept leaking when pressure was applied on tying to the 'D' rings with chains.

It was noticeable that our flight sergeant did not accompany us to Kenya. Whilst in Nairobi, I wrote to my car insurance company in Nicosia transferring my policy from fully comprehensive to third party fire and theft. I did this on both attachments to Nairobi, saved myself some money. Before leaving Nairobi on each occasion I wrote informing of my return and asked for the policy to be reinstated to fully comprehensive.

After three months, the other NEAFMAMS team came out to take over from us and do their stint, loading all those 44-gallon drums of aviation gasoline. So now we could make our way back to Cyprus.

## Back to Nicosia, 1966

Our flight back to Cyprus from Nairobi was in one of the returning Britannia aircraft on its way back to its base in RAF Lyneham. We were on our way to RAF El Adem in Libya, a transit and refuelling stop, and also where we got off to connect for a flight to Cyprus. I recall this flight took hours and hours to get there; it had to circle for quite some time over Libya as a sandstorm was affecting visibility and could have caused problems if sand had got ingested within the aircraft's engines. Having finally landed, on getting off the aircraft I then found that we had to offload our own baggage from the hold.

A few days waiting, in transit accommodation, for the weekly Hastings of 70 squadron with its weekly supplies, and then we were flown back to Nicosia. When at last Lita and I managed to say hello, she told me of an incident that had really upset her. Being very lonely, she had made herself known to some of the other wives who were in the same situation as her. A gathering of them assembled in the house of a girl who was heavily pregnant. Her husband (a Senior Aircraftsman MAMS bloke) had been taken off flying duties as a result. There were five wives waiting for the pregnant girl's husband to come home.

Please bear in mind that he had nothing to do other than sit around in our section. All the other section personnel were away. He came home during this meeting and Lita asked him if there was any mail for her and the others, as he was the only person who was authorized to collect mail at that time. Would you believe it – he said 'Yes, but I didn't know you would be coming around to our house'!

The effect this had on Lita and the other wives is beyond imagining. She and another of the wives got a taxi and presented themselves to the Postal Clerk in the Army Postal Service collection room at RAF Nicosia; the army clerk confirmed that there was mail for them, but he would not issue it to them, as they did not have an authorization chitty for mail collection. These poor girls did not know what to do, or who to speak to to get this sorted. They were much perplexed at all this and I can assure you it had a terrible effect on the other wives too. There were many tears shed over this, and getting hold of our pay as well. There was much talk of going back to the UK, because they had no one to turn to when we were away. The rest of us did not allow this airman to live this down, to such an extent that he wanted off the section, a request which I am pleased to say was granted.

At the first opportunity I really let go at our CO about this sort of thing. I asked him, 'What are you going to do about looking after the wives, when we are not there?' Boy did I hate that bloke! During my three years in Cyprus I had four different commanding officers; a lot of the other ranks couldn't stand the work ethics and got themselves transferred onto an easier lifestyle.

On returning we had a three-month wait before another detachment to Nairobi. During this time we were tasked to fly to Tehran in Iran and Ankara in Turkey to deliver 'diplomatic mail'. Because of the distances these were always at least a one-night stop, sometimes more. 'Diplomatic mail' was carried in white padlocked mail sacks, although there were occasions when very large consignments were transported.

Lita had a Spanish passport, which was only valid for five years at a time and needed to be renewed whilst we were out there. I found that the Spanish consular official was a lady married to a Greek Cypriot, living on a farm some distance off the main road between Nicosia and Famagusta. We set off to find the place. The road map showed a road leading off towards a farm, so we gingerly approached the farm along a long winding dirt track, not knowing if it was the right place or not. No signage anywhere, but fortunately it was the right place.

The lady said the passport would have to be sent to the Spanish Embassy in Beirut for renewal. This would take about three weeks. This meant that Lita was without official identification. It also meant that we had to make two journeys to and from this isolated farm to collect the renewed passport, because the local mail service, we were advised, was not to be trusted with these documents.

To ease this situation, Lita accepted the fact that she would be better off getting a British passport, which we arranged; mind you, in Cyprus this was not an easy thing to do. It culminated with a visit to a 'Notary Public', making her swear allegiance to the Queen and Country on a bible. Then we had to cross his palm with silver.

During the coming weeks we did not see much of our flight sergeant, the one who had said he was the section admin officer. It seemed that he still lived in his married quarter in Akrotiri; perhaps he knew something we didn't? It became a topic of conversation between us; the CO wouldn't talk about it.

My wife was having a bit of a medical problem and after consultation with the Station Sick Quarters Medical Officer, it was decided that she needed an operation, which had to be carried out at the Army base at Dheklelia, where there was a large army contingent together with a huge hospital. It was a 35-mile journey along a roadway that had previously been notorious for hijackings.

I just don't know how I would have coped if I had not got transport, as she was in dock for about a week. I picked her up and brought her home and she showed me what they had done. Well, I fainted at the sight – her body from the neck down to the waist was black with bruising. In all the other similar procedures she has had since, for the same reason, nothing resembled the after-effects from that group of Army butchers. Incidentally no follow-up visits or procedures were offered. We just had to get on with it.

Another incident that will not shake itself from memory. We had experienced a rather physically and mentally-demanding day. The team was on detachment back at Akrotiri and the wives were still in Nicosia. Whilst trying to get cleaned up and have something to eat, I was visited by a duty 'snoop' (An affectionate term for an RAF policeman) who came and found me and told me to report to our CO at Akrotiri Air Movements section. So off I walked the

GERRY DAVIS

mile or so, and met him there. It must have been about 2100 hours. He told me that Lita had earlier that morning been admitted to Station Sick Quarters at Nicosia. He had phoned the Senior Medical Officer (SMO) to ask him how and why she had been admitted. As a result of this conversation he thought the situation did not warrant me being sent back, as in his opinion and the SMO's it wasn't serious enough. He then said that if I wanted to borrow the section Land Rover I could, but he wanted me back for 0600 the next morning, although by now it was gone 2300 hrs.

He had known about this for some time, but why he thought I was indispensable was beyond me. Remember it was about a 150-mile round trip. At that time there was no motorway, and the roads were not all that special. I asked him if he would drive me. I was tired and had been working physically hard all that day and did not feel up to it. He said no, of course. I bloody knew he wouldn't, but I wanted to put him in a spot. Boy, did I hate that swine. I weighed up the situation and decided that if I went I would not come back. I asked him what he would have done if it had been his wife. He said he would have stayed!

Not many wives would, or in fact did, put up with this. Bear in mind that those who lived in married quarters had wives' clubs, social events and much more contact with other Brits.

My wife had only seen me for short periods in the time we had been out there. She was depressed and lonely, and had been put into a situation where she felt abandoned in a foreign country with no one to turn to for assistance.

Fortunately one of the other wives happened to visit her and got her to Station Sick Quarters at Nicosia. Remember Lita had had to wait three months before joining me. In a three-week period we then had two homes in two different Cypriot towns, and I was in a job which necessitated flying off throughout the Middle East at short notice, with indeterminate periods away without any forms of communication.

When I was off duty Lita and I explored much of the north-eastern part of Cyprus, which at that time was under the control of the Turkish Cypriots, as far as the 'panhandle' and the lovely beaches. This meant we had to go through several road blocks, manned by either Greek Cypriot National Guard or the equivalent local Turkish armed guards. These road blocks were several hundred yards apart, with stretches of no man's land in between. We often had to get out of the car whilst it was searched, although I must mention that both sides were always very polite.

We also liked to eat out as much as possible. On one of these occasions we ate in a Nicosia restaurant which was owned or was managed, by Mandy Rice Davies of the Profumo affair fame. She was married to an El Al air steward. In another restaurant we met the famous South American group Los Indios, famed for their song 'Maria Elena'. The group consisted of a family, father, mother and two sons. They kept coming to our table especially to speak to Lita in Spanish. They found out that her Christian names were Maria Dolores, which was also the name of one of their songs, and they sang it at our table, all playing their guitars. During the interval they all joined us at our table, which was quite nice. The two sons took up our offer to come home with us for some supper.

The main street through the city was called Ledra Street, also referred to as 'Murder Mile'. It was where in 1956, several British soldiers were shot dead, just because they were British. Three seconded British policemen were also shot – two died and one was severely wounded with five bullets in him. Several army wives were also shot whilst out shopping.

A good way along this narrow street inside this walled city was the 'Green Line,' a United Nations-patrolled area which divided the two warring sides. A roadway large enough for a Land Rover was ploughed through houses along this line, enabling the UN to patrol and hopefully keep the peace. It was noticeable that there seemed to be several tavernas within easy reach of both side of the Green Line, occupied by youngish men of both nationalities, who it appeared could at the slightest hint of trouble produce their weapons and fire away at each other. Lita and I had some lovely photos taken in a cellar along this street.

Three months up, we had to go back to Nairobi to relieve our other team.

## Back on the 'Oil Lift' at Nairobi (Embakasi Airport)

We set off from Nicosia in a Hastings aircraft of 70 Squadron to El Adem, to await onward movement to Nairobi in a Britannia aircraft en route from Lyneham to Nairobi. On arrival, we soon got back into the swing of things. We again took up residence in the Spread Eagle Hotel.

The six Britannia aircraft were each still doing two sorties a day, loaded with 56 44-gallon drums of aviation gasoline and flying between 0500 hours and 2200 hours. On their return flights to Embakasi they often brought back 90 empty drums from the two airfields of Lusaka and Endola, although the majority of the drums were transported over land. The vehicles used were large Fiat lorries with trailers. These vehicles transversed the jungle tracks which often had to be made as they drove along. When it rained they often got stuck in the mud, with other African drivers helping each other to get unstuck. On arrival the drums were then checked to see if they were still suitable for air transportation, and if they were they were refilled.

I noted that amongst the African labourers who assisted us in working on the aircraft were some familiar faces, and many new ones too.

Time off was spent exploring the pleasures of the Kenyan capital. Those of us who had a taste for some ale soon developed a liking for the local brew, of Tusker beer. You had to down gallons of the stuff to dull the effects of those barrels of oil and get rid of the stink of fuel.

One thing worth a mention – on one of our days off three of us decided to partake in a mission to find an Italian nosh house. Well, to be honest, I fancied a spaghetti bolognese. So there we were ambling down Jomo Kenyatta Avenue in the capital city of Nairobi with our sergeant in the middle when a gorgeous young English lady stopped right in front of our already red-faced SNCO. Placing her hand on his chest, in a very sexy voice she asked him 'Would you like to come to my flat and listen to music for the afternoon?' The look on his face suggested an imminent heart attack. He spluttered out something to the effect that he was in a hurry and had to get back to work. Well I never, and he was single too!

At this time the film 'Cowboys in Africa' was being made, and we often saw some of the stars relaxing in the Thorn Tree Café of the Stanley Hotel.

Another place we often visited between shifts was the large market, where nearly all the stalls and shops were owned by the large Indian merchant classes. This of course was before the mass exodus from Kenya, as a result of all the Asians being affected by the new laws brought in in 1968, forbidding them to own businesses.

I bought several wooden carvings and some decent books. Back at our hotel I haggled with one of the African wood carvers for a couple of days for a two-foot-high carving of a Masai warrior standing on one leg holding a spear and a shield. It was stained to look like ebony, which he claimed it was. Anyway he eventually settled for the equivalent of £2. This carving takes pride of place in our living room fireplace even today.

As the corporal on the team, I was the only one who had a definite job to carry out (actually this job was carried out throughout my time on MAMS). I was responsible for all the paperwork, the driving of the specialist vehicles and trimming the aircraft. On the Oil Lift this also meant driving the 12000lb fork-lift, operating the lift platform, loading and helping to tie down the barrels of gasoline. There was a standard method of chaining these barrels down to the aircraft floor. The paperwork consisted of freight and passenger manifests, six copies of each. There was also a form Sigs 52 to be sent to the forward airfield and command HQ, informing them of the aircraft loads. All the RAF aircraft had a separate trim sheet; all these documents were very large, consisting of three different coloured copies, with duplicating paper in between. On these forms a graph was drawn, indicating the position by weight of the loads in marked areas of the freight bay. At the bottom of the forms was a box which the trimming of the aircraft was to fall within, for the aircraft to fly safely. Quite a lot to do within the turnround time so that the flight schedules could be met.

To help carry all the paperwork and associated paraphernalia, I was issued with a 'nav bag'. This was a sort of large briefcase, naturally blue in keeping with the RAF colours, and I also had an Omega service watch.

You may have noticed that my first year in Cyprus involved a lot of travelling; I was away from my wife for nine months as well as other shorter detachments. Our time spent together in that first year I reckoned to be no more than three weeks, not all in one go.

I was supposed to be on an accompanied tour! How Lita stomached it all was beyond me. Some of the wives didn't, and this was when the cracks started to emerge in the morale of the section as a whole.

Another three months passed, and it was soon back to Cyprus.

## Back to Nicosia

Lita was again pleased to see me, not having known the exact date or time when I would get to our bungalow in Ayios Dhometrios in Nicosia. I had only been home for a few hours, getting updated by her on what had transpired in her time on her own while I was away, when there was a loud banging on the door. It was an RAF policeman. I manage to put a pair of shorts on to answer it. He said, 'Corporal Davis, report back to work immediately, you're wanted for another detachment!' Or words to that effect. I had to travel with him in a Land Rover back to base, taking my kit with me, as I wasn't coming home again that day.

This also happened another time; I'll come onto that later.

We were tasked to fly to Tehran in Iran to deliver 'diplomatic mail', a three-day affair, then back again for a one-day debriefing and general sorting out of kit and catching up with our laundry etc. That's when Lita told me that the other corporal's wife had given her husband an ultimatum - get off MAMS or she was going back to the UK. He made representations to the CO.

In the meantime we were informed that we as a unit, together with all other RAF personnel, including 70 Squadron and their Hastings aircraft, were being posted back to RAF Akrotiri. The powers that be had decided to close down the RAF station at Nicosia. This meant another round of house hunting in Limassol.

Off we went travelling the 70-odd miles, house hunting again. Lita and I settled on a ground floor flat with a lockable garage. With the closure of RAF Nicosia, it was interesting to note that all the Cypriot businesses, supermarkets and shops etc upped sticks and moved their businesses to Limassol.

There were many detachments throughout the Middle East; I shall attempt to enlighten you about some of the incidents that transpired whist serving on them.

We as a team seemed to spend an awful lot of time in North Africa, mostly at Benghazi and El Aden (Tobruk). We went on one 'fruit and veg' run to El Adem one time in a Hastings aircraft. There was six of us, the officer, the flight sergeant, the sergeant, myself, the corporal, and the two airmen. When we arrived and offloaded the aircraft, we were greeted with a signal from Command HQ at RAF Episkopi stating that we had to stay in Libya to await further instructions.

We settled in to wait. The instructions came a few days later. Our officer told us that he had been ordered to fly to Malta to be a witness in a smuggling court martial, because he had been a passenger on the flight the arrested servicemen had been on, so he disappeared off into the blue yonder. Then our illustrious flight sergeant received notification that his wife was in the RAF Hospital on the Akrotiri peninsula, so off he went back to base. It later transpired that on one of her usual shopping trips to Limassol, she may have stopped off at one or two of the many watering holes for some local lubrication, and on her 18-mile bus trip home the Cypriot driver thought it proper to eject her for causing altercations with the other passengers. In the process she broke one of her ankles.

That left the sergeant, the two lads and me sweating it out at El Adem. Shortly after that we were ordered to board a Pembroke aircraft for two destinations, Idris and Benghazi. We first landed at the farthest destination, which was RAF Idris, formerly known as

RAF Castel Benito. This base was in the process of closing down as an RAF station and there was only a skeleton detachment of RAF personnel left.

The two lads and the sergeant were tasked to load two Hastings aircraft with the last of the essential equipment destined for Cyprus. While we were waiting for the aircraft to be refuelled, we all went to get some refreshments. It was noticeable that the entire domestic site of the empty RAF camp was being ransacked by the local Arab populace for all movable furnishings. There were lorries, donkeys and camels with trailers, all loaded with purloined abandoned goods. The sergeant, by the way, was most displeased at being left with the two lads. After all he, would have to do all the paperwork and assist them in their plight, instead of standing around looking pretty as usual.

Shortly after refuelling was completed I boarded the Pembroke for Benghazi. Yes, all on my lonesome. I was told that I had to assist the Loadmaster of an arriving Beverley aircraft, which was coming in fully loaded with supplies for the British Army garrison and taking out returning cargo for the UK. I was also to arrange labour for this turnaround with the local aircraft handling agent, and hire a forklift. On completion of this task, the Beverley was to drop me off in Malta, so that I could catch the first flight back to Cyprus.

On landing, the pilot of the Pembroke lost no time in taking off again for his base at El Adem. I ambled over the aircraft parking area trying to find the handling agent's shed. I eventually found it and made myself known to the Indian gent who was in charge of the apron workforce. He confirmed that he had a forklift, although on inspection it seemed to have been left there by Noah after the Ark had sailed.

By this time midday had passed and I had a further couple of hours to wait for the Beverley to arrive. In the meantime a 3-ton army lorry arrived, driven by an Arab, who was accompanied by an Army staff sergeant complete with his red sash and underarm stick. I introduced myself to him, although I immediately got the impression that he looked upon me, being RAF and only a corporal, as something akin to dog poo on his shoes. I humbly suggested that he should have the vehicle offloaded so that it could be driven up to the aircraft directly for offloading. His response was, 'You had better get on with it then!' So I thought to myself, OK then buddy, you will have to sort it out yourself when I have gone.

The aircraft arrived, and I thought yippee, other RAF types to talk to. I was in for a shock there too. I met the Loadmaster, a Master Loadmaster (Warrant Officer). He said that he and the rest of the crew were going for something to eat; I asked him if he was going to assist me in the turnaround with the freight. He said 'That's your job, sunshine', and departed.

I also spoke to the Captain before he left for his meal and asked if he was aware that I was to be dropped off in Malta. He asked for the loading weight for take-off, which I worked out quickly and gave him. He then calculated that he had sufficient fuel to go straight to Abingdon, their base, as they were expected that night at some function or other. He said 'You can either come with us to Abingdon or stay here, after all it's my aircraft'. He did not want to stop in Malta as he knew there would be further loading onto his aircraft, which would take him over the flying duty hours, and they would then have to night stop.

I wasn't having that - I wanted to get back to Cyprus. I asked the handling agent for help, which he kindly offered, although he stated that his priorities lay with their scheduled services. I also went to the communications signals office, to send a signal to my HQ at Episkopi In Cyprus, pleading with them to get the original plan to drop me off in Malta confirmed to the aircraft captain. I did not want to go back to the UK, as I knew I would be stuck in limbo awaiting an air passage back to Cyprus, which might take days, or possibly longer.

The offloading started, but every time a civilian aircraft landed all the Arab labour disappeared. I struggled on with off-loading the lightweight stuff onto the ground, awaiting the return of the forklift. Which never came back. I had to go and ask for help again, overall about five times. This was really frustrating.

Eventually all the freight was off and I got the 3-tonner reversed up to the aircraft and started the loading. When all was on, I began tying it all down. By now I was sweating profusely and helped myself to the aircraft's flasks of cool water. During this the army staff sergeant got rather aggressive with me, as he wanted his lorry loaded so that he could get off. I suggested that he contact the handling agent and hire his manpower when we had gone. I further mentioned that he might want to move the unloaded freight father away from the aircraft, as we were about to start engines. He nearly burst a blood vessel at this. I suppose he did not have authorization to hire civilian labour. Tough!

When the crew arrived back, the Army staff sergeant had a go at the crew to let them know how uncooperative I was, but they were not in the slightest bit interested. The crew went for briefing and to collect the weather etc. They came back as I was still securing the load and had masses more to do. The captain asked me if I had signalled HQ Episkopi, and I said yes. He shouted to the rest of the crew. 'We have to stop over in Malta to drop this corporal off!'

Again I had become very unpopular. By this time I realized that I had not eaten all day, so I asked the loadmaster if I could have something to eat on the flight or when I had finished tying down. He said 'I haven't catered for any passengers, I'll see what I can do'. I mentioned to the Loadmaster that I had not finished tying down.

He said 'go upstairs and get a seat for take-off then, finish off when we are airborne'.

I came back down after ten minutes or so and asked again for something to eat. He pointed to an aircraft flask which contained lukewarm water and said, 'make yourself some soup!' That was all I was offered.

This tale is not over yet. On landing at RAF Luqa in Malta, I identified myself to the Duty Air Movements Officer (DAMO), asking when the next flight to Cyprus would be. 'Ah! A MAMS bloke' he said. 'You won't get away for several days as there's a backlog of passengers to go. So I want you to give us a hand with our aircraft turnarounds as we are short of staff.'

I thought the situation could not get any worse. I was skint, tired, fed up and very hungry, and no one was at all interested in my plight.

Eventually I did get airborne for Cyprus, in an Andover aircraft. I was seated at the very rear of the aircraft by the ramp, amongst mail bags. It was freezing sitting there. After a while I went forward to use the loo, and as soon as I moved a couple of feet the warmth of the aircraft heating system hit me, much to my relief.

On landing I was met by our CO, who told me to get back to the section first thing the next morning for another trip. I tried to explain all the goings on I had experienced, but he was not the slightest bit interested.

At least Lita was pleased to see me when I finally got home.

I actually loved that job, but I had reached a decision that I would complete my contract in the RAF and leave. The only thing that mattered to most people in the RAF was what was on their shoulders and what they could get away with.

I often wondered if others in this Royal Air Force had to endure all that I was experiencing.

## Back at RAF Akrotiri

It was now 1966. A lot had happened in our first year, and those days and the following time served in Cyprus are clearly etched in both Lita's mind and mine.

Settling back into the routines at Akrotiri, there were many detachments and changes of personnel to come. The situation with the CO and the flight sergeant came to a head. I don't actually know all the ins and outs, only the bits that concerned me. We hadn't seen much of this flight sergeant; he always seemed to be missing from the section. On the occasions when he was present, he seemed to be having lots of 'behind closed doors' discussions with the CO.

It became obvious that he wanted off the section. Actually he was totally unsuited for the position he occupied. He obviously did not intend to get his hands dirty at any cost. He also tried to keep away from the CO as much as possible. He was actually an embarrassment to our unit.

This situation with the CO went on for a bit, until one day the flight sergeant did not turn up for work. The CO told me to go to his married quarter to find out what was up! I drove there, and when I found the address, he was outside the house and gave me the greeting, 'What the f★★★ do you want? I've been posted to Episkopi, and that's where I'm off now!'

Oh dear, I could just see that sparks were going to fly. I got back to the section and reported my findings to our CO. Understandably he was not best pleased at hearing this. Building up to a crescendo, he then told me to go back and get him. At this, I respectfully asked him not to include me further in these negotiations. The CO slammed the door of his office, whereupon we could all hear the telephone conversations that followed.

Incidentally we minions were chuffed at the flight sergeant's exit from the unit.

His replacement was another flight sergeant, a tallish gent who sported one of those under-nose hairy things called a moustache. This man was a one off. No, it was not the case of the mould being broken when he was born; it must have been broken before he came from it. We gave him the nickname of 'Bo Diddly', not to his face of course. His wife, by the way, was of a similar disposition, although he had a daughter, and as time passed, one of our number was giving her an occasional 'free service', much to the displeasure of her dad.

Shortly after settling in from the UK and after his wife had joined him three months later, she received notification that she had been left a large sum of money. I presume her finances had never before been gazumped by such a large wad of readies. Being the person she was, she did not believe it, so she had the money transferred to Cyprus so that she could hold it and count it, after which it was dispatched back to the UK.

He had his old car shipped out to Cyprus, and for the amount he paid in shipping costs he could have bought a new one in Cyprus. He was very proud of this machine. It happened to pass that one day when there was not much on, and he happened to visit a thunder box establishment, one of those places where you had a handle dangling on an attached chain, presumably to stop others pinching it. So those of us of the unwashed variety (well me actually) thought that we would take advantage of his absence. We took one of his cherished car's metal hub caps off and placed two smallish pebbles inside. Honest it made a lovely sound, just as if the engine was wasted. He was beside himself with worry when he started off for home that afternoon. That was until someone later that day suggested what the real reason for the noise was. It was funny while it lasted though.

One day in the early hours of the morning, before the 'crack of sparrows', we were hauled out of our abodes to load a Hastings aircraft. On arrival at the aircraft there was no lighting on, so we made a journey to the Aircraft Servicing Flight (ASF) for someone to provide this for us. We couldn't find anyone at all. They must have been hiding in their cubby holes fast asleep. Well, our esteemed Flight sergeant made us start loading by using his torch, which (like him) was very dim. We were getting stuck into loading this aircraft when all of a sudden the aircraft door opened and a rather posh voice said, 'What going on here then?'

Old Bo shone his torch round and found himself looking at the face of the Akrotiri Station Commander. He stood bolt upright to salute and stand to attention, in the process hitting his head on a bracket protecting a light fitting, which resulted in his cap badge piercing his forehead. Blood pouring down his face, he tried to give an explanation to the senior officer, accompanied by the emission of copious amounts of spit, as to why we were working in the dark, something not uncommon to us I might add. The Station Commander departed, and would you believe it, a collection of Aircraft Servicing Flight personnel suddenly appeared as if from their slumbers in haste and provided us with lighting. I bet there was a follow up about this later in the day.

Several of the staff, all ranks included, even one of the officers, wanted off the section for a variety of reasons, mostly because of the CO's bullying attitude and the fact that time in Cyprus was very limited, due to the many off-island detachments. One of the Lads, an LAC, an Anglo-Indian chap called Keith, had pestered the CO for a transfer off the section, to anywhere! He had his many requests denied. We got the impression that the CO was worried about what the powers that be thought of him, with all and sundry wanting off MAMS; Keith was a lovely lad but was continually being picked on by the four SNCOs and the officers, mainly because he was at the bottom of the pile.

It came to a head when a detachment was coming off and our passports had to be shown, mainly at hotel receptions. (Don't get the idea that when on detachment we had luxurious accommodation, some of these places were absolutely horrible.) The CO got us together for a briefing and said, 'Make sure your passports are up to date, as they will be required for the next detachment'. Keith blurted out 'mine's out of date sir.' The CO went ballistic, and shouted 'Get it renewed now, and that's an ORDER!' Well Keith really excelled himself in his next utterance. He announced to us all, especially the CO, that he was an Indian national, that there was no Indian Embassy in Cyprus, and he did not wish to renew it!

Guess what? He got his wish and was transferred off MAMS onto Station Movements that afternoon.

For a short time there were 13 on the section; two officers, two flight sergeants, two sergeants, three corporals and four airmen, making up two teams. The additional corporal was a ground engineering fitter. He was most useful at our base at Akrotiri in starting up ground power units, attaching trolly-acks (mobile batteries) for aircraft lighting and servicing and operating the Britannia freight lift platform. He was also taking care of the daily inspections for the Land Rovers and the Massey Ferguson tractor/forklift. He looked after anything technical which happened to crop up, like cleaning out the blocked floor tie-down points on Britannias. He took pride in the fact that he was a skilled technician. It wasn't long before he sought to leave us, as in his opinion there was not a need for his expertise, and he often suggested that his skills were needed elsewhere rather than amongst a bunch of labourers. Before joining us, throughout his service career, he had never worked outside normal office hours. He felt that being with us was not fair on his prospects for advancement within his trade, and kept in regular contact with the Ground Engineering section at Akrotiri, as he knew several of them through the courses for his trade and the previous postings he had been on.

He was also an international football referee, which he had a great passion for, attending many of the local games in this capacity, including of course the Cypriot international games. Because of this he was well known in the top brass echelon throughout Akrotiri and Episkopi. He was a likeable person and I personally got on well with him. He lived in a married quarter in Berengaria, a suburb of Limassol, with his wife and two kids.

The problems for him really got under way when a detachment came up for El Adem. The boss told him he was coming with us. He asked in what capacity he would be needed as he pointed out that he was a fitter and not an Air Mover. Well, the boss told him that he was unsure of the actual requirement, but he was coming anyway. He came, complete with his tool kit, but there was, as expected, nothing of a technical nature for him to get involved in. The boss told him to give us a hand in loading/unloading and chaining down.

That's when the fireworks started. He was livid, and remonstrated with the boss that he had been brought on a detachment under a false pretext away from his family and other commitments which he had had to put off. Furthermore, there was nothing of a technical nature for him to do. He also pointed out that he did not think it fair that two of the team, SNCOs, were required to supervise him and he did not know how to chain loads. He did not wish to learn, and definitely was not interested in becoming an Air Movements coolie.

This excellent trained fitter, baffled as to why he had been attached to NEAF MAMS in the first place, was beside himself with anger. Of course the boss wasn't standing for this, which carried on when we got back to base. I think there must have been lots of paperwork flying about, because it wasn't long before our fitter left us. We didn't even have the chance to say goodbye. He got his wish and went back to the Ground Engineering Section. He was not replaced.

The corporal on the other team was replaced by Ken; he also lived in Limassol in a flat with his wife and baby daughter (our goddaughter). There was some trouble with one of his neighbours in the multi-service block of flats where he lived, a man who on several occasions caused a lot of disturbance with shouting and knocking his wife about. This always seemed to happen when he arrived home late at night roaring drunk. He was also in the RAF. It came to a head one night after violent abusive shouting coupled with banging of doors and screaming of his battered wife. So Ken, being the nice lad he is, thought he might pop over to see if he could help in any way.

Well off he went with the best of intentions. He knocked on their door to be greeted by a very drunk, angry, swearing individual telling him to seek intercourse and travel far away, or words to that effect. At which good old Ken, who might have taken slight umbrage, asked him, 'would you mind keeping the noise down?'

I understand that in the next few moments the proceedings did not go to either's plan. An exchange of fisticuffs took place. Well this flat dweller did not realize who he had taken on, and as Ken was administering several volleys of the 'old one two' one of this bloke's ears flew off. How the bloody hell was Ken to know that this individual had a false ear?

The matter did not end there, as the one-eared wife-beater called the Military Police (MPs). Ken later that night had a wonderful reception at the MP HQ in Limassol. He might have mentioned that the bread and water wasn't that bad.

I previously mentioned that I had bought a new car. As servicemen in Cyprus we had a special deal, in that we did not pay the local tax on cars. Incidentally I bought the top of the range model and our next CO bought the basic version. When I was away Lita used to sit in it and rev up, just for something to do!

This tax thing was something to do with serving in the Sovereign Base Area. You could sell it to another serviceman, but if you tried to sell it to a Cypriot, there was the tax to pay. This also applied to cars being written off, as they no longer belonged to a serviceman. The Commanding Officer of 70 Squadron soon found this out (by this time 70 squadron had converted to Argosy aircraft) when he totally smashed his car up. He of course did not want to pay an extortionate tax bill on his expensive car, so to overcome this technicality, he chose to export the wreckage. We were then involved in loading the battered car onto a pallet and placing it on board an Argosy. He duly had the export documents signed by the customs people and got airborne. He flew about for a bit, found a nice spot somewhere out there in the Mediterranean, opened the rear doors and oops, it fell out. Job done!

Because I had to spend a lot of time away from Cyprus, Lita decide to seek nursing work in the RAF Hospital on the Akrotiri peninsula, and she worked there for about two years. She was getting really fed up with all my absences, so she thought that as she had got to know the surgeons very well, she would organize an operation on my nose. I had been experiencing breathing difficulties which had developed whilst I was serving in Nairobi, and wasn't getting any better. It happened all of a sudden, just as we were off again on anther jaunt. Our CO received a phone call, virtually as we were about to board the plane, informing me that I was to report to Princess Mary's RAF Hospital. This meant of course that I would be taken off flying for a period of three months. He was livid. I was chuffed!

She had used her friendship/acquaintance with the ENT surgeon (A Wing Commander) to seek his help in bringing forward my stay in hospital. He agreed to her request after learning that I was off again into the wild blue yonder. Influence, it seems, does work!

Lita was on night duty at the PMRAF Hospital one night during a very heavy storm. The next morning as she was on her early morning rounds, she looked out of one of the windows to see a ship on the beach which had been washed ashore during the night.

I was in hospital for about a week and then I had a fortnight's sick leave, during which Lita and I explored a lot of ancient Cyprus. There is so much to see. A lot of the history of the early Mediterranean is there to view, and you can wonder at the complexity of their skills in building and engineering. I was fascinated to visit the many sites which can be explored to learn of the wonders of those early civilizations, which include the Palaeolithic period, the Khirokitia culture, the Phoenicians and the Crusaders, together with the Romans, Greeks and Turks, and not forgetting the British. Whenever the opportunity arose to explore the many wonders that could be viewed, we took it.

On getting back to work, I was greeted by the CO, who told me that as I was unable to take any detachments that involved flying for three months, I was being sent to RAF Episkopi on detachment. RAF Episkopi was mostly a headquarters camp, where all the brass had their offices. Although there was no airfield at this base, there was a collection of Bloodhound missiles on the massive parade ground; they were huge. I got to know them at close quarters, as every six months we loaded and unloaded them onto and off Belfast aircraft. At Episkopi I had to report to our Movements Task officer, the gent who dished out our orders and detachments, a Flight Lieutenant Harry Pollard.

Five years later, after he retired from the RAF as a Squadron Leader, Pollard and I shared an office at Bristol Airport and became firm friends. When we first met in his office at Episkopi, he said he had to go somewhere urgently and left the office with me in it and locked the door! Years later, when I asked him about this, he told me he had had an urgent need to visit the toilet and had to lock the door for security reasons. With me in it! I never let him live that one down.

I had to urgently replace two corporals, one Army and one RAF. They had become friends, and their wives had become friends. It went on from there, culminating in a wife-swap arrangement, which resulted in one of the ladies refusing to go back to her husband. It finished up with one of them having the privilege of looking after two ladies. One of the corporals thought this wasn't fair, so the two corporals squared up to each other in this office and a fierce exchange of knuckles ensued, during which a great deal of the office furniture was rearranged and redistributed, much to the annoyance of those caught up in this melee. The powers that be were not amused. All the parties involved were sent back to the UK and charges were initiated against the two corporals. I was sent to make up the loss of manpower, until others were posted out from the UK. Was I glad when those six weeks were up.

When I got back to the section we were sent on a detachment back to Nicosia. Not only that but I had to drive our Massey Ferguson T21 tractor, a modified version of the agricultural variety, with a set of forks attached at the front and a ballast box on the rear. Nicosia, as you may recall, was about 70 miles away. I had to drive this vehicle in the scorching heat of the midday sun. It did not have a canopy and I was instructed not to stop en route because a lot of vehicles had been stolen or hijacked on this road. Of course when all was completed at Nicosia, I had to drive the thing back to Akrotiri.

During my three months on the ground, there was still plenty to do in Akrotiri. I remember we had to give a demonstration of assembling a Britannia Freight Lift Platform (BFLP) to a senior officer, a group captain. This machine was totally air portable, and could be assembled and disassembled by a team of 'highly trained' air movers in a short time. But on the day of our demonstration at Akrotiri, it all went wrong. We started off OK and assembled the thing, until it came to connecting the auxiliary power supply and operating the machine to raise and lower. It went up all right, but a safety bracket had been left in place and when lowered it made an awful crunch, much to the annoyance and embarrassment of the flying officer who was in charge of us. He was a nice chap who was on a short service commission (five years). He was constantly being picked on by our illustrious flight lieutenant and eagerly awaited his return to UK and demob.

Every now and then the local police in Limassol would carry out a dog shoot. This was necessary because packs of dogs roamed around causing mayhem. They would raid dustbins, chase and kill other animals and frighten just about everybody. The police would use shotguns to do this, load the dead animals onto trailers and dump them in monsoon ditches on the outskirts of town, then set fire to them. This would cause further problems as other dogs would then feed on the remains. Our dog Kim once or twice came into contact with some of these packs. He would return covered in bites and what could only be described as other dogs' love juice. He looked as though he had won the lottery.

Above our flat lived an RAF chief technician (equivalent to a flight sergeant) and his wife, who never engaged in conversation and kept to themselves. We could hear the constant rows between them. One night Lita and I were sitting on our balcony enjoying a glass of wine and the sunset, when all of a sudden we got soaked to the skin. The tenant in the flat above had thrown a bucket of water over his patio, presumably to wash ants off. Our protests and the knocking on his door were not answered. They became adept at avoiding us.

## Beirut

We were tasked to fly to Amman in Jordan, as part of a delegation which was involved in trying to sell Lightning aircraft to the Jordanian air force. We set off after loading a Blackburn Beverley aircraft with a Lightning aircraft pack-up, consisting of spare wheels, specialist tools and other assorted equipment, along with a huge circular compressed liquid oxygen container and a couple of missiles.

The Beverley had its huge rear clam-shell doors taken off as a precaution in case there was an emergency situation whereby the oxygen container had to be jettisoned. We took along two army lads, air dispatchers, ie specialists in unloading goods whilst airborne. The jet fighters had already flown to Amman.

About an hour into the flight I noticed that one of the engines had feathered and the prop had stopped. We were told that we would have to divert to the nearest airfield, which happened to be Beirut International Airport. After landing, we were informed that one of the engines was unserviceable because of the type of load we were carrying, which included some missiles. Some of us would have to stay and guard the aircraft. Fortunately for me and the two lads, the two army air dispatchers volunteered for this.

We were in Beirut for four days awaiting the arrival of another aircraft to transfer our load onto, which eventually turned out to be an Argosy. We were transported to a hotel on the waterfront, organized by the embassy Air Attaché. I had to share a room with a lad called Seamus – a nickname we christened him with, as he originated from Northern Ireland. He was a lovely fellow. His Nan sent him Mars bars regularly. No wonder he was covered in spots.

The first night in this hotel, the evening entertainment was Scottish country dancing. It was amazing to witness all the Scottish expatriates arriving from throughout Lebanon for this event, all wearing their individual clan kilts. Even swords were produced and laid on the floor for dancing.

The next day both Seamus and I were told to book out of the hotel and make our way to another. It was pretty obvious to us why, being at the bottom of the ranking pile, although the reason given was that a Royal Navy ship had entered port and our accommodation had previously been booked for them.

We had to make our own way to this other hotel after being given guidance as to where it was, about 500 yards through the Arab quarter on 'Shanks's pony.'

So off we went, both struggling with our kit through the streets. We happened to pass by an Arab gent who had a sword. I said 'Good morning Abdul,' to which he seemed to take offence, as he drew his sword and waved it at us. We quickened our pace as best we could and made haste to our new billet. He followed us for some time, scaring the daylights out of us, shouting and gesturing with his sword. It was a great big thing, honest.

On arrival at the hotel we booked in, got the room sorted and proceed back to the other hotel to meet up with the others for something to eat (we had to eat there with the others for all our meals), worrying about our Arab friend and whether our kit would still be there on our return. As we had a while to wait for a relief aircraft to rescue us, we all chipped in to hire a taxi to see the sights, and enjoyed a day out. There is of course much ancient history to view near the capital, and our driver, who spoke good English, seemed quite knowledgeable. It was worth the money.

On returning to the hotel, it was getting quite late, and both Seamus and I were thoroughly knackered. We had to share a large double bed, which had a long light flex dangling down from the ceiling with one of those push button switches. I said to Seamus, 'You ready for the lights out?' 'Yep' he replied, so I pressed the switch and electrocuted the pair of us, both of us started screaming like banshees. No one came to our rescue though.

I bought a lovely gold bracelet for Lita here. Our holiday soon over, it was back to work and greet the arriving Argosy, and those two Army lads who had spent all that time out there on that warm apron guarding our aircraft. They could not have done much anyway as they did not have anything to defend themselves with. So after changing the loads over between the two aircraft, the Beverley departed on three engines empty and we left on the Argosy, both the aircraft returning to Akrotiri.

The total exercise was a flop, as the Jordanians bought American fighters anyway. We incidentally had a bet that they would buy American jets. They probably got them for nothing.

## Benghazi

We as a MAMS team also spent a lot of time in Benghazi, where we were regular visitors. On the very first visit the two SNCOs and we three lads had to seek overnight accommodation with the Army in one of their camps, which was originally built by the Italians long before the war, and was called D'Aosta Barracks. After signing out a rather clapped-out Army vehicle, our CO booked into a hotel in Benghazi, over 20 miles away. As the driver I had to take him there and collect him the next day. We all went with him, so as to know where he was staying, then we drove back to the army camp to find some accommodation for ourselves, altogether a round trip of 50 or so miles. Here he collected a very generous daily allowance, but only ate a packet of biscuits.

On our arrival at D'Aosta Barracks, our two SNCOs disappeared into the sergeants' mess. I had to book the vehicle into a compound for security reasons, and then seek a duty lance corporal for our transit billet accommodation. It was quite dark by now and we were dog tired. We had to sign for three iron beds, which had seen better days, and were issued with two blankets and three well-soiled mattress biscuits each. We then struggled with all this and our kit, although we did borrow a handcart, with a long 'T' handle, then trudge a lengthy distance to an old tin hut. This hut had double wooden doors which would not close properly due to their age and because a whacking great pile of sand was blocking them. It was padlocked with a chain going through holes in both doors. There was one dim light inside, and the roof was riddled with holes, through which the stars were very visible.

I said to the lance corporal, 'Can you please find our two senior sergeants, as I am refusing to stay here.' He disappeared and shortly came back with an Army warrant officer, who said, in the usual authoritarian loud voice 'What do you Brylcreem boys want, hotel accommodation? If it's good enough for our boys, it's good enough for you lot'. Not the sort of person you could negotiate with.

The ablutions were about a hundred yards away. By now it was past midnight and we had been working and travelling and could hardly stand up with tiredness; we also had an early start in the morning. So we bedded down as best we could.

In the morning we went through the same trudging to get rid of the bedding and the beds. We three made our way to the cookhouse for something to eat, only to find out that all the squaddies had their own mess tins and their own knives, forks and spoons. We had nothing to drink with either. All we ate was a greasy egg placed between two slices of dried bread. One of the serving cooks lent us a rather bashed tin mug, which we shared between us so to satisfy our raging thirsts with copious amounts of what the Army called tea.

Inside that mess hall we felt like animals on display. Because we were RAF it was an opportunity for most of those squaddies to help themselves to a large portion of piss-taking and cat-calling.

Outside, while making our way to collect the vehicle, we met our two illustrious SNCOs. They wanted to know why we were taking our time, and why were we late getting the vehicle. I actually honed up on all my known collection of expletives at this point. I must admit that with the help of the other two lads, we could not help ourselves in describing how we felt let down by these two.

Collecting the officer from his luxurious bivouac, I might have mentioned that we were slightly distressed and could he please get us something to drink. He resorted to the usual stance of 'This is not the time or place to discuss this, corporal'. We were on our way by now to the airfield to turn around several aircraft. I then respectfully asked our flight sergeant, whilst in the vehicle, if he would mind asking the CO, who he was sitting next to, if he would give consideration to us three being transferred off MAMS, and could we now go home please, as we felt that no one cared what happened to us.

The CO exploded. 'Speak to me later corporal!'

'Thank you sir. When we get to the airfield can we please have something to eat?'

He said, 'I have some biscuits in my bag, if you want them corporal?'

That's how we knew about his diet. It went silent from then onwards.

The officer, by the way, on all these trips, carried an imprest to pay for his own expenses and any sundry costs that may have arisen. Of course if he did not spend his daily allowance, he pocketed it.

Later when back at base he told me that from now on, after authorization from Command Headquarters, we would be staying in hotels when on trips where there was no RAF accommodation,

I have left out an awful lot, but I fear you may get the impression that most of the time we excelled in whingeing. But how would you have felt?

Whilst on further visits to Benghazi, the first time in a hotel, we could not stomach any of the offered meals. So it was arranged, after some discussion with the CO, that we would stay in one hotel and eat in another, in fact the one he was staying in, although he would not dine or spend time with us while he was away, and kept to himself.

We got into the habit of taking our own supplies of 'lubrication', mostly a crate of 24 cans of Tennents' beer, to be shared between us three lads, although it usually disappeared on the first night.

One time in our shared room, on the second floor, we had a balcony; it gave an excellent view of the tower block five feet away. During the course of a stormy night we soon got rid of the ale, together with some Cypriot wine we had brought. During the course of that night we three lads had as good at time as we could make of it.

We felt privileged, in that we had two visits from the Greek hotel manager; it was difficult for us to comprehend why he came to our room to see us, as we did not think the noise that we were making was excessive. We thought he was after some of our ale or wanted to join the party. Lovely guy though.

Much later, after the three of us got our heads down in the large bed, I was awakened by the noise of the wind and rain howling away, so I decided to get out of bed and close the curtains, to help stop the rain coming in. Incidentally the balcony doors would not shut. On grabbing both the curtains and giving them a good yank, the large wooden heavy pelmet came off the wall, hitting me on the forehead, knocking me out. I lay there for most of the night, eventually waking soaking wet as the rain had flooded the room.

This 10th class establishment only had the water turned on for a four-hour period in the afternoons, which incidentally was never when we were there. So if you wanted to flush the loo or have a wash outside these hours, tough!

Our flight sergeant, 'Bo Diddly', was with us; incidentally he was a stickler for service etiquette, insisting on being called Flight Sergeant instead of 'Chiefy'. Being off duty, he really did not know how to behave and wanted to be with us all the time and take charge of everything. Unfortunately for him we did not want anything to do with him on our time off.

During another trip to Benghazi, while we were having a few days' respite to await the return of several aircraft, we dossed down in the same hotel. This particular day was lovely, so we thought we three lads would venture out onto the waterfront and do a spot of fishing. I had taken some hooks and line for this purpose. So we pinched some bread from our breakfast table, in the other hotel, to use as bait.

Just as we were leaving we came across our two SNCOs. 'Where you lot off to?' asked the sergeant.

'We're going fishing.'

'OK if I join you?' he asked.

'What you doing today, Chiefy?' I asked.

'Don't call me Chiefy,' was his reply.

'OK Chiefy' I replied, 'see you later!'

'Hang on a minute' he said. 'Can I join you lot, Corp?'

'Don't call me Corp!' I replied.

I then suggested that we all have a vote. 'Who wants to have a lovely day spent with the flight sergeant?' I asked.

No one put their hands up.

'Sorry Chiefy, no takers, you're on your own!'

So off we go. This of course did not stop old Bo; he proceeded to follow us at about 30 paces behind.

We had gone on along the waterfront seeking a goodly place, as it were, to cast our nets. He was still following us, so I suggested that we run. Off we went. Shortly after setting off we heard this loud screech from behind. Stopping to investigate, we espied old Bo dancing about grasping one of his boots. He had started running as well, and in the process he had run onto a large nail which had gone through his bondu boot and into his foot. In his uncontrolled hopscotching and prancing about he managed to hit his head on an overhanging palm tree, stabbing himself. What a sight! Holding onto one of his boots with one hand and the other hand grasping his head… if only we'd had a video camera to have recorded this event for posterity!

It was rather unfortunate that we four could not control our laughter. In actual fact we became hysterical. He was shouting his head off, telling us to stop laughing and help him out. Unfortunately this option would never have been considered.

It was rather sad really, though I might add that he had never shown a modicum of care or respect for anyone other than himself.

We didn't give a shit for him, and went about enjoying our day out. No, we did not catch any fish either.

'Gosh!' we said to ourselves, 'no one is ever going to believe this in years to come!'

We finished off the day devouring copious amounts of laughing juice, and by the day's end, we were thoroughly pissed. Old Bo turned up the next day at the breakfast table with plasters on his head and limping, which set us all off again. He was a bit upset at this and the whole incident, so he resulted to his usual, well, it's hard to describe, but when he was raged up, every word was accompanied with a shower of spittle. The CO thought it was funny too.

How this man had progressed throughout his service career was beyond belief. The other stations he had served on must have had him promoted to get rid of him.

## El Adem

As previously mentioned, we always seemed to be going to the desert outpost at El Adem. It got to the stage when we started taking frozen meat and other goods, including fruit and vegetables, and we made up a sort of box which we could take frozen items in. Our contact was the Air Movements Warrant Officer, who was one of the Duty Air Movements Officers (DAMOs). He used to give us a list and we would do our best to get the stuff for him. He then sold it on, after paying us and taking what he wanted of course. This worked OK for a while.

In return we expected to be billeted in one of the transit Tyneham huts at the rear of the air movement's buildings. Initially we had to share accommodation with loads of squaddies in huge billets, or stay in tents. Squaddies, especially when laced with copious amounts of 'laughing juice', always seemed to want to start fights and being close to them was like sharing a cage with a pride of hungry lions. You would be trying to get some kip, and they would probably start to sing the SAS song or one of their own regimental concoctions. Which meant that before the song had ended you had better be standing up and naked or you would get done over, probably by as many as could get hold of you. If you were able to get to sleep when this happened, you hoped that someone would wake you. This even took place in the NAAFI.

One time we were sitting outside the NAAFI on a sort of veranda, having a beer, when in the distance we saw a cloud of dust. It became evident that this was a squadron of Ferret armoured cars, four of them, racing towards where we were in this veranda. They were going fast and it transpired that they were not going to slow down either, so we 'blue jobs' decided to evacuate from where we were sitting. We were just in time as they ploughed through the three-foot high wall surrounding the place, scattering and driving over the chairs and tables. They stopped just short of the doors to the NAAFI. Apparently they had a bet on as to who would be the first to sink ale in the NAAFI.

We arrived another time for a big exercise, a sort of war game. There were many aircraft there, including loads of Army and RAF personnel. We arrived with the usual goods for sale and asked the Warrant Officer if we could have our usual Tyneham hut. He said 'no!' We had to go find an empty tent on the football field. (Field is a loose description, there wasn't any grass around.) After this we did not take any more goodies to El Adem. Incidentally we did manage to sell on the goodies that we brought.

We settled on a tent, marked T7. There was not a lot of time off on this detachment, and we three lads came back to the tent one day to find a squaddie in residence. It later transpired that he was a godsend.

Deserts are funny places, hot as hell in the daytime and near freezing at night. In the wintertime we wore the normal UK uniform. In the summer it was KD (khaki drill). It also rained like hell, with thunder and lightning, and torrential downpours flooded vast areas. The water had nowhere to go, as our part of the desert was hard ground, with a dusting of sand and pebbles, so when it got windy you had better shield your eyes. Sand got everywhere, in your eyes, ears, especially up your nose, in your kit and clothing. Then there were the flies and other bugs to contend with.

Not only all this, but you could not wander outside the marked area of the camp as the whole area was riddled with WWII mines from three forces, the Germans, the Italians and the British. There were still occasions when wandering Arabs stepped on one and departed off to Valhalla to seek the 'forty vestal virgins'. That is of course why wandering Arabs always allow their women to go ahead of them in the desert.

Just to mention the toilets, they had flush toilets, a sort of collection of half a dozen sit-downs in a block for hundreds of airmen/squaddies. They actually had Arabs who maintained these establishments. What I mean is, they sat outside and either prayed or slept all day. These toilets were disgusting, always blocked with brown effluent and vomit, generously displayed all over the walls and floors, presumably by servicemen, who either couldn't or wouldn't dare go near the sit-downs.

I purloined a spade and got into the habit of seeking a quiet spot before the flies started patrols at first light, to satisfy my ablutions. Honest, it was gross. Getting back to this exercise, long hours and really physical hard work, without proper sleep or food was taking its toll on us. We had to have short breaks between aircraft, and although the cookhouse served food throughout the 24 hours it was always fry ups. Eating this had a terrible effect on the bowels and wind manufacturing. Farting became a sport, something I had learnt about on previous detachments and postings.

During one of the stormy downpours, I got permission for us three lads to see if our tent was still standing. I drove the Land Rover and eventually found the tent; it was difficult to find in the dark with all the ground being flooded. Driving in flooded areas was doubly difficult, as you could not make out if you were on a road or track. The Army chap who shared our tent had the forethought to stack all the canvas beds on top of each other, putting our kit at the top of the pile. It was already soaking wet. I said 'kit', most of it had been stolen anyway.

We gathered up what was left of our kit and took it with us to our office, which was a marquee without sides. From then onwards, for the next two weeks, we slept either in the Land Rover, on aircraft night stopping or anywhere really, even in the crowded Air Movements building. That was until one night when I was in a state of complete exhaustion. I was shaken into life by an unknown sergeant who ordered me to drive a civilian chap over to the other side of the airfield to what was known as 'German Town.' This was a collection of buildings occupied by former German soldiers, who at the war's end did not want to be repatriated to their homelands in the Eastern Block. They helped built the German war cemetery, in the shape of a castle, overlooking the Tobruk Harbour; the inside of this building is beautiful. They also had jobs within the RAF camp in various trades.

When the British were asked to leave Libya, those still alive were flown to Cyprus. They were stateless citizens, as far as I know. These German fellows also drove around in one of their WWII utility vehicles, which it seemed was still going well. Lita actually met some of these guys when she was nursing in the Princess

Mary's Hospital on the Akrotiri peninsula - they came from Libya as patients, mostly with liver problems.

I took the opportunity to explore as much of the surrounding area as possible. I was very aware of the fighting and the WWII battles that took place, and visited some of these sites. On the way from the RAF airfield at El Adem to Tobruk there are four cemeteries, commemorating the Commonwealth, French, English and the Italians who gave their lives during those days of war. The Commonwealth, French and English ones are kept in an immaculate condition, but it was sad to see the treatment the Italian site had received. It had been desecrated, and the whole site had been laid to ruin, with all the headstones and other memorials smashed.

Surprisingly there was a lot to see, for instance, the tank trenches, the barbed wire defences, and scattered in various sites many large guns. On entering the town of Tobruk on a long white-painted wall, there was a collection on display of paintings of the British regiments' insignia.

The Germans had a castle-like structure built high up overlooking the harbour. Inside, as a centrepiece, was a water fountain, which unfortunately was not at that time functioning and in need of maintenance. All the names of their war dead, no ranks, were inscribed around the inside walls. The French one was laid out to form the Cross of Lorraine.

## Kufra

Another place which was often on our stopping list was Kufra, some 500 miles or so inland in the middle of the Sahara. This was a deserted bombed-out desert airfield built by the Italians and captured by the Free French and the Long Range Desert Group during WWII. There was a bit of a shindig at the Fort of El Tag, after which the Italians and their African soldiers surrendered. In actual fact it was an oasis, which started off as a 'captured slave' holding station for desert caravans heading north and east.

The airfield was marked out with 44-gallon drums painted black and white, and our pilot on each occasion had to do a low pass over the site to scare any loose camels or goats off the runway. The site was scattered with the debris of the war, and there was a shell of a bombed-out hangar, bits of aircraft and burnt-out vehicles. All useful equipment had long since been scavenged or purloined by the local populace.

Our mission there was to transport members of the Special Air service (SAS) on training jaunts on desert survival, from and to El Adem. They took their specialist 'Pink Panther' Land Rovers with them. These vehicles were loaded by us onto a Beverley; about 10 days or so later we would fly back to retrieve them and their vehicles. One of their training sorties was to find their way 120 miles north to the site of the 'Lady Be Good,' a wartime B24 Consolidated Liberator bomber, which famously ran out of fuel on returning from a bombing mission over Italy and crashed in the Libyan Desert, due to poor navigation and bad weather. The nine crew members all died. The wreckage was first discovered by an oil surveying aircraft in 1958; all the bodies were found in 1960. There have been several books written and a film made of this tragic wartime incident. The remaining wreckage of the aircraft was removed by the Libyan authorities in 1994 to the Libyan Air Force base of Jamal Abdel Nasser, formally called RAF El Adem. This was to stop the vandalism and thieving of the remaining artefacts. Yes sir, way out there in the desert!

## Got Al Arfaq

Another Libyan Desert airstrip I spent time at was Got Al Afraq, on the north Libyan Mediterranean coast. It was a flattened site, amazingly close to the sea, and was I believe specially prepared for this exercise. I understand it carried on for several months after I left. I have looked several times on Google Earth for its exact location, but I think the desert may have reclaimed it back, or its name has been changed, or something else.

The aircraft I recall being involved in this adventure were Beverleys and Argosys. It was a war game, involving paratroopers being dropped to capture the airfield and the RAF regiment and other Army troops defending. Accommodation, of course, was tents; we were supposed to dig trenches for when we were being attacked by aircraft or by paratroopers, but because of the amazingly hard ground all that was done was to place two-inch white lashing tape to mark out where they would have been dug out. When an attack took place we had to down tools, as it were, and stand in between the tapes.

Whenever an aircraft took off or landed, the sand that was thrown up obliterated the whole area, covering everything and everybody with sand and grit. On the few occasions when we had a stand down, we sat in the sea to cool off, and the clouds of sand whipped up from the aircraft still managed to reach us. Even when bathing in the sea, amazingly, you would still be sweating.

We were issued with bars of special soap, which was supposed to assist us in personal hygiene and for doing our laundry with. It was like scrubbing yourself with a stone.

Way out there in what could be described as 'no man's land' we had Arab visitors trying to sell eggs! It truly is amazing how they would suddenly appear from nowhere in this way out place.

This exercise has a place in RAF history, because one of our aircraft crashed there. It happened on 7th May 1968, when I had already left. It was an Argosy XR 133. The aircraft was departing for El Adem with an empty freight bay, save for six army paratroopers, and with a crew of five, total souls on board eleven. An enterprising Army sergeant had built a shower cubicle by the runway, actually a large, heavy erect wooden lamp-post type pole supported by another pole, with a 44-gallon drum secured at its top. I understand a pump was arranged to replenish the sea water. He had assembled them to one side of the end of the runway at a height no greater than twelve feet, so after releasing a valve it gave a shower of sea water. The Argosy aircraft captain took off rather sharpish and banked steeply at a very low height. As he did so his wingtip hit the drum and the aircraft cartwheeled. It burst into a massive fireball, killing all on board and totally destroying the aircraft.

## Ankara

I mentioned earlier the diplomatic mail trips we used to have to go on. These were flown with 70 Squadron, who until November 1967 operated Hastings aircraft. They then converted to Argosys, with better payloads, a much easier aircraft to load, having a flat cargo bay.

The two frequently-visited destinations in the Hastings were Tehran in Iran and Ankara in Turkey. Each time we landed at Ankara we were met by an RAF airman from the British Embassy, wearing civilian clothes. He was a senior aircraftman of the motor transport trade (an SAC MT driver). He happened to be a fluent Turkish speaker, as he had married a Turkish lady whilst out there. Although he was used on occasion to serving as an interpreter, he was very worried, as his RAF engagement was coming to an end and he was unsure as to what his future was going to hold. He wanted to stay out there as a civilian, but wasn't receiving any positive feedback from his embassy bosses.

He gave us the address of the American Forces SNCOs' club in the city, which we visited each time we went there. On one occasion we arrived there in a taxi when all my associates opened their doors and scampered off, leaving me to pay the bill. Which was fine in itself, but the taxi driver had obviously been in situations like this previously, and to ensure he was going to get his money he stuck a screw driver into my stomach and relieved me of all my cash. My so-say comrades thought this was very funny, although they eventually coughed up their share of the fare.

Steaks were the order of the day on the menu, although my T-bone had to be sent back three times; even so, it was still red in the middle. Whenever we went there we were pestered by the club staff for buying their PX duty-free goods, like cigarettes and whisky.

Tehran

Tehran was the other frequently-visited city. I went there many times, both in Hastings and Beverleys. I was always fascinated on our aircraft's final approach on landing at this airport, as we flew over a massive collection of military hardware, which seemed to stretch for miles.

One time we took a Rolls Royce in a Beverley. On landing, the embassy staff was there to meet us, and they had another Rolls Royce for us to load and take back to Cyprus for repairs. I had noticed on the flight out to Tehran that we had on board another passenger, who kept to himself. I presumed that because he was wearing flying overalls he was a spare aircrew member.

All was going well and we offloaded the Rolls from the aircraft; the one to go back with us was nearby. The chauffeur who had brought it to the airfield insisted on reversing it on board the aircraft. Well OK, no problem there. During this the local BOAC agent, who acted as our agent as well, was kept busy by the other embassy staff to one side of the aircraft sorting out the paperwork, out of view of the loading. He was an Iranian gent, who was also our go-between for accommodation, refuelling etc and a general nosey parker at that. Nothing wrong with that either, although I did notice that our mysterious passenger and the chauffeur seemed to know each other, as they hurriedly swapped clothes. The newly-kitted-out chauffeur walked off the aircraft and got into the Roller, followed by other embassy staff, and off they drove. I thought to myself, aye aye, so that's how it's done, James Bond and all that. It seemed that an exchange of secret personnel had just taken place.

The BOAC handling agent, whose name I have forgotten, always wanted us to take over bottles of whisky, which he would buy from us for a small profit, and then sell on for a larger one. We bought ordinary whisky in Cyprus for 10 shillings, while Haig's Dimple and other malts were £1. He always warned us that we could only sell it to him, and if we tried to smuggle it for sale to anyone else he would have us arrested. His cousins worked for the customs authority, or so he said. Anyway I was happy with this arrangement.

Another time we were in Tehran when a big joint exercise with the Iranian forces was under way. There were a lot of the RAF aircraft there, including Canberra bombers with their aircrew and ground crews. We all knew the Canberra had a large bomb bay, which was also used for carrying freight and other stuff - in this particular case, crates of whisky. The BOAC agent found out and offered to buy the lot from them at his one-offer no-haggling price.

The two pilots may have suggested to him that he should go away and make love. Well did you ever! He got his cousins over and the two pilots were arrested and their 'liquid refreshments' confiscated. This later resulted in these two being court-martialled in Cyprus.

When we were there we stayed in a hotel called the Miramar. As I understand it that should mean 'sea view'. The only view in all directions was a mountain range. I remember the bar in this hotel served Watney's Red Barrel and was frequented by a lot of expatriates, two of whom were ladies. Later I was to learn that the elder one, by a year or so, was married to an English Iranian Airways flight engineer, while the other was his daughter from a previous marriage. These two ladies, after a chatty evening and the sampling of much beer, invited two of our number back to their flat for a nightcap, or two or three.

Early the next morning these two RAF buddies were making their way back to the hotel on foot. There weren't as it happens too many locals about at that time, except for an Iranian policeman wearing jackboots, a white helmet, a blue shirt and a white webbing belt and gun holster, which they saw walking towards them. He drew his pistol and indicated that they should raise their hands and turn around and face the wall, whereupon he frisked them, relieving them of the contents of their wallets, watches, rings etc. I was given to understand that this incident scared the pants off them, especially as they said, the previous night had been wonderful.

## Special mission

In the first week of June 1967 we were tasked to deliver urgently-needed equipment to an unknown destination. We often had these sorts of tasks where we didn't know where we were going, or for how long. This was a last-minute thing and detailed in invisible, quick–fading ink, I believe. It all started about 0400 hours with a knocking on my flat door in Limassol by two military policemen, telling me to 'get to work ASAP!' There could not have been any misunderstanding on the faces of these individuals. Conversations with military policemen are best avoided whenever possible.

They waited the allotted two minutes for me to pack, and all the while I was trying to reassure the missus that I wouldn't be long – she said that she had heard that one before. Then I was off on the 18-mile journey from my private accommodation in Limassol to Akrotiri, closely escorted by these two MPs, one RAF and one Army, travelling at breakneck speed.

The cargo we had to load, I was led to believe, had been taken off a ship in Famagusta. On its arrival at Akrotiri no time was wasted in loading a considerable number of wooden crates, all marked 'FRAGILE' and with vague descriptions of the contents stencilled all about their sides, onto an Argosy of 70 Squadron. While all this was going on we were being watched by loads of 'brass', who looked as though they had been dragged out of their beds as well.

I asked the boss where we were going so I could enter the destination on the aircraft trim sheet. He said, 'Leave it blank'. We found out whilst airborne that our destination was possibly somewhere off the coast of the Mediterranean – 'need to know,' and all that stuff.

I thought to myself, where else could it be within easy flying distance from Cyprus? I hoped we were going to keep away from the four nations that were having a bit of a fracas (the six-day Israeli war, June 1967). I remember that it was a very bumpy ride; well I suppose that one could expect that, given that the aircraft didn't seem to get much higher than the waves it was flying over. We eventually did climb up a bit so as not to hit the land and continued to fly very low until landing at our destination. (Much later I found out that we landed at what was then called Lod Airport.) On landing, the aircraft engines were kept running and the rear doors were opened while we were still moving. Vehicles were waiting for us and the several tons of cargo disappeared onto them in less time it takes to shake a stick, and soon we were airborne again. From our landing to take off was about 15 minutes.

Same thing on the way back to Cyprus, we flew at wave top height. I later read about this in the English press, which said that no British military aircraft were involved in the six-day war. At this time, it was reported that a transport aircraft leaving Cyprus had flight planned to go to Athens, but had returned to its base at Akrotiri, for technical reasons!

## Homeward bound

We had a new CO, a smashing chap who was quite different from the others, although he did like a drink or two. I was on my way through Limassol to Akrotiri one morning, driving my car, when I spotted him trying to extract himself from a monsoon ditch at the side of the road. He was thoroughly Brahms and Liszt. He had also been robbed. I managed to get him into the car and take him to his married quarter. He snored all the way there. His wife was not too pleased to see him.

I then went onto the section, where our flight sergeant (Bo Diddly) was in charge. I thought I would keep quiet about the boss that was until HQ Episkopi kept ringing up to speak to our CO. It must have been urgent, because they kept ringing. So I told Bo what had transpired on my way into work that morning and said I had delivered him to his married quarter. I also mentioned that it was no use going to get him as he was totally out of it. This of course did not stop the phone calls from Episkopi. Watching old

Bo trying to make excuses on the phone as to the whereabouts of our CO was epic. His making feeble excuses in staccato, trying to defend the boss and giving false promises as to when he would phone back, was an experience far better than going to a comedy show. That phone must have needed to be sanitized after all his utterances.

This CO of ours was admitted to the hospital later, into the ward Lita worked in. She found it very embarrassing telling his wife not to try and smuggle whisky into the ward.

1968 arrived and the detachments kept coming. As Akrotiri was a very busy airfield, it was decided that the runway needed to be resurfaced. That meant that all operational personnel and the squadrons of aircraft would be sent to Nicosia International Airport. That included us. This carried on for the first few months of the year. The road between the two airfields was constantly being used by RAF personnel going to and fro, especially by the married chaps whose wives were still living in Akrotiri and Limassol. On a weekend off we were travelling back along the road to Nicosia and got stuck behind an overloaded lorry, full to the gunwales with sacks of potatoes, presumably on its way to the docks. The lorry was really struggling to maintain speed as the gradients increased, so much so that it could hardly make it up these slopes. At one of these it was moving at a snail's pace and making a lot of engine noise.

I noticed that one of the sacks did not look secured and thought it might fall off, so I asked one of the lads if he could help secure it better. He got out of the Land Rover, walked up to the lorry and tried to adjust this one sack, which funnily enough fell into his arms. Oh how shocked we were. I suggested that he should place it in the back of our vehicle, and then we would try to catch the lorry up and tell the driver.

As we overtook the lorry we all gestured to the driver, trying to tell him what had happened. He just waved and kept going. Those spuds by the way were delicious!

Nearing the end of my three years in Cyprus I made application that I may be granted a posting to RAF Lyneham, as I wanted to keep my hand in, as it were, within the Air Movements trade as it was my intention to leave the RAF and seek employment in civil aviation in a similar capacity on completion of my 15 years' total service. There was a procedure to apply for a 'last tour of duty posting' for those whose contracts were coming to an end.

I was also petrified that I might be posted for my last three years in the RAF back to a stores unit. Although that's what my original trade training was all about, I had honestly forgotten all I had learnt. Thankfully my application for a final tour of duty posting was approved.

In my last month on the island and after just getting back from North Africa, I asked for time off to help Lita do the final packing and finalize the selling of my car and other things that needed to be done, including finding a good home for our dog Kim. I also managed to pack some wooden packing cases in which to send our possessions home. Would you believe the boss said I was needed for another detachment? It was taking place in the north east of Cyprus at a landing strip near the Army base at Dhekelia, which was called Kingsfield. I flew there in an Argosy with our Land Rover and eventually, three days before I was due to leave Cyprus, I drove back. This took a whole day of driving, and by the time I handed in the vehicle to a secure compound at Akrotiri I was fed up, I can tell you. Then there was the long journey home to Limassol. Lita by this time had given Kim to an RAF policeman and his family, which was quite upsetting too. I sold my lovely mint condition car to one of our flight sergeants, who had a hell of a job borrowing the money.

Our Cypriot landlady was also upset, not I presume because we were leaving, but because she would be losing rent.

Eventually the day came for our departure. I had mixed feelings about leaving the Island, although Lita had spent more time there than I had.

We arrived at the Air Movements Terminal to find that there was no one there to see us off, as all our people were away. On boarding the RAF Britannia aircraft and on getting to the top of the steps, we were about half way amongst the 115 passengers. I looked down to see that there was an almighty row going on between two Air Movements lads, both of whom we knew. They were exchanging punches and blasphemy. I said to Lita, 'what a fine departure we are having!' Finally we boarded the Britannia for RAF Lyneham, leaving it all behind. We set off for dear old England not knowing what our future would bring.

# CHAPTER 7

# RAF LYNEHAM, JUNE 1968

~~~

On landing at RAF Lyneham, Lita and I were met by my mother, who had arranged for my Uncle Harry to pick us up in his car. We then drove on to Bristol, to my mum and dad's house in St George. Lita and I had already booked a passage from Southampton to Vigo on the SS *Begonia*. After a week with my mum and dad we got the train to Southampton for the onward sea journey to Spain to meet Lita's parents. Lita by this time was three months pregnant.

Eventually we got on the ship, porters carried our baggage to the cabin, and as I was looking for change to give them a tip I turned round to see Lita being sick in the sink. We hadn't set sail at this point! When we did, I had to get the ship's doctor as Lita was not feeling too good at all.

The ship was going onwards to the West Indies, and had many passengers to take across the Atlantic. On setting sail, I thought I would find a nice spot to watch the boat leave the dock, so I went well forward and got myself a wonderful view. As the ship started leaving the ship's hooter sounded. The noise was ear shattering, and went on for what seemed like ages.

Our first port of call in Spain was La Coruna. Lita's dad knew we were on this ship and that the first stop in Spain was La Coruna; then the ship was going onto Vigo, where we were supposed to get off, then across the Atlantic. He knew the ins and outs of shipping, being a second engineer on a cargo boat, so when he arrived at La Coruna and the docks he arranged for us to be offloaded so he could meet us. It was quite a surprise for Lita and me when the ship got alongside the dock to see her father talking to a Guardia civil sergeant, who incidentally was a relation of his. All the other meeters and greeters were behind barriers. We got off the ship to be told that our baggage would be going onto Vigo. This resulted in much heated consultation with many people, which, happily for us, was successfully resolved and our baggage was offloaded.

Lita's parents' house was a three-hour drive from the docks, along the dusty roads, amongst some of the most beautiful Spanish coastal panoramic views. Not like now with the modern highways, courtesy of European Union funding. On arriving at the house I was pleased to see how close it was to the sea, with a beautiful beach which curved away into the far distance.

We stayed in Spain for six weeks, Lita rekindling acquaintance with many friends and relations; of course I was introduced to lots of people without knowing what was being said, not being a Spanish speaker. Eventually, our holiday over, we got on board the same ship on its return trip from the West Indies. Our return ticket was from Vigo, so that's where we got on board.

On arrival at Southampton, we made our way to the railway station and were told what platform the Bristol train would be leaving from. It was quite a challenge for me to carry all the cases over the bridge to this platform, as Lita was not in the best of health. Neither was I, as coming over on the SS *Begonia* I had slept near an open porthole and got myself a bad back and neck pain. However, we managed to get there in time. But then a train pulled in on the opposite platform on the other side of this bridge, and we heard an announcement that it was the Bristol train. What a panic! I shouted for assistance to a porter on the other platform, who eventually met us half way and got us on board the train. What a mess up. It took quite a while for us two to settle down. Good old British Rail, eh?

We spent another week with my mum and dad before I had to report for my last three years of service at RAF Lyneham. I did get permission for Lita to stay with them until I could get accommodation for both of us organized. I was not sure whether or not Mum was OK with this.

I arrived at RAF Lyneham on a Sunday in July of 1968; naturally it was raining. Lyneham was the main RAF transport base, and at that time there were squadrons of Britannias, Hercules and Comet aircraft based there. I found out which barrack block was allocated to the Air Movements people, got myself some bedding, found a room and moved in. My official arrivals date was the next morning. Being a Sunday there were not many airmen around, as they were all either at work or off for the weekend. I did not know any of the airmen that I saw.

The rain by now was really belting down. I managed to find my way to the Pegasus Restaurant, in other words the Airman's Mess, and got myself a meal. This mess by the way had won many awards for its splendid cuisine.

I entered the NAAFI club for a look around, not seeing anyone there who I knew either. So feeling a bit fed up, not knowing what was in store for me at my new station, I thought I would try my luck in the local pub. I asked around to see if there was any way of getting there other than going the long way round past the main guardroom, and someone suggested taking a short cut through the St Michael and All Angels Church of England graveyard. This churchyard backed on to the camp boundary and had a gate leading to and from the camp. I was pointed in the right direction and off I went. By now the area was quite muddy and squelchy.

While I was crossing this field in the pouring rain, I saw some conduits in straight lines which had had their protective concrete slabs placed to one side. Inside were central heating pipes at a depth of about four feet, which were in the process of being relagged. They were slowly filling up with rain water.

When I got to the graveyard gate I found that the padlock on the gate had been broken, and the gate was easily opened. I made my way through the churchyard to the main road, turned left and walked up the Calne road to the junction with the B4069. Then I turned left and the White Hart pub was just a few yards further on.

There were not many people in, all locals. As I was getting into my second half gallon, a chap mentioned, after looking out of one of the widows, that the car park was flooded and he had better get off home while he could.

The sky was flashing with lightning and the rain was really belting down. This chap opened the door and water flooded into the pub, straight down into the cellar, which was filling up nicely, with a noisy roar and cascading of water. The landlord got quite worried and so was I. I thought that from now on I had better drink bottled beer.

Soon the remaining customers were having to stand on chairs, the water in the pub bar being about four inches deep, and the landlord declared that he was shutting the pub. I got outside onto the main road, attempting to paddle my way through the torrent of water created by the slope of the road. I was amazed, even though the haze of the local brew, how deep the water had become in such a short time. It was difficult to identify the centre of the road. I eventually made it to the church, where the water was even deeper, got through the gate into the camp and made a beeline for the Air Movements block; it was of course pitch black. Then, crash, bang wallop! I disappeared down a flooded conduit. My first thought as I came up for air was how lovely and warm the water was. Gosh did it stink! It was mixed like thick brown soup with rust from the pipes and the remnants of the lagging material. It tasted lousy too.

Then to my horror I discovered that I could not get out, so a minor panic ensued. I eventually did get out, after considerable effort, as the water was higher than the top of the conduit, and paddled, squelched and tumbled my way back to the billet block. The way I looked, I would have scared the pants off Dracula. I got under the shower fully dressed, with my overcoat on, trying to wash the filth off layer by layer. My clothes and I were in a bad way. It sobered me up though!

I dumped all my clothes in a smelly pile in the drying room, thinking I would try and wash them at a later date. I felt secure in the knowledge that no one would pinch any of them. There was no chance of buying any new clothes, as even in those days £10 a week didn't go very far.

I got up early the next day, prepared myself in smart clean battledress, and after some grub, made my way to the Station Headquarters to start the arrivals procedure. You are given a blue arrivals card, and you then have to go around the camp getting signatures on it so that you are entered on all the important section records. But first, a visit to the Station Warrant Officer for the usual bull about dress, saluting, and amongst other things, station duties.

There were half a dozen of us new boys assembled for his indoctrination. The Warrant Officer started off asking about the previous night's rain and if it had affected any of us. I stupidly told him of my misfortune in taking a midnight plunge whilst walking through the churchyard. Big mistake! He asked if I had been wearing uniform or civilian clothes. As I was in civilian clothes it was all right then. Not quite. He promptly put me on Orderly Corporal for taking an unauthorized short cut out of and into the camp.

So started my first day at RAF Lyneham, and my last three years for Queen and Country. Imagine how I felt. One of the three shifts of the Strategic Air Movements section (A Shift) was lucky enough to have me allocated to them. At that time there were two air movements sections, either side of the airfield, designated as Strategic and Tactical. Eventually the Britannias and Comets moved onto RAF Brize Norton, and the air movements were reduced to one section.

During the arrivals processing I applied for married accommodation, either RAF hiring's or married quarters. I kept checking with the married family's office, who allocated the married accommodation; I had to wait four or five weeks before I heard of anything being available. Then I was offered a hiring in Malmesbury, some nine miles away. Not having any transport at the time, I thought that was a bit far.

I was speaking to one of the other lads on the same shift as me who knew the area well, and he offered to take me there and show me around, but he didn't have transport either. He suggested that we could borrow a mate's new motorcycle, which he did. Off we went to Malmesbury, with me on the pillion. We managed to find the house OK, but I was not comfortable with it or the area, so we started back to camp. About halfway back the engine on this borrowed motorbike seized up and we became stranded, not knowing what to do. We decided to hitch a ride as best we could and proceeded to wave our thumbs at all the passing cars. Well would you believe a passing driver in his Land Rover stopped, asked us what was up, told us to load the bike on the back and drove us back to the camp!

On reaching our destination, we thanked the kind driver. We then had a long walk pushing the bike to our section and taking it back to its owner. I didn't witness the explanation given to the owner of the bike, but I was told that he would get it sorted.

Shortly after I was offered a married quarter at a place called Compton Bassett. I thought where the hell is that? I was taken there in an RAF car to view the house, which was at a long-closed RAF station about three miles from Calne and six miles from Lyneham. All the buildings had been pulled down save for the 100 or so married quarters.

I accepted the house, after confirming that there was a regular RAF bus service to and from Lyneham so that I could get to work. When I took it over the previous tenant was there; as it happens I had served with him in Bahrain on the same shift. He had now been posted off somewhere else.

The Warrant Officer, Families Officer, inspected the whole house and found fault with the cooker and the toilet. He told the previous tenant that he would be docked £4 from his pay to give to me, so that cleaning materials could be bought. The tenant was livid.

At this site there was a small families' NAAFI shop, a Barrack Wardens store and a public phone box, which was constantly being robbed, and that was it.

As soon as I could I collected Lita from Bristol and we journeyed on the bus to our new house. By this time she was over five months pregnant and hadn't seen a doctor. We were at this time eager to get ourselves sorted and settled down to a reasonable lifestyle as a married couple, which had been denied us up to now because of my job.

I began the tedious and repetitive process of trying to catch the bus to and from work, which did not always run, causing frustration with phone calls to find out why. Very often I was not able to make a call because the phone box had been vandalized. Oh the joys of it all! At this time my pay was about £16 per week, out of which the rent of £3 10s was deducted. I saved up as best I could so that I could buy a car, which happened to be a clapped-out old Austin A35 van. The hooter didn't work and the battery was knackered, together with loads of other unaffordable things which needed urgent attention. Money, money, money!

I settled down to a routine at Lyneham, initially working only on Britannia aircraft and using and driving the specialist vehicles such as the aforementioned Britannia Freight Lift Platform (BFLP), the Condec, a specialist large American-built vehicle for moving palletized loads about, and the 12000lb lift forklift.

I was on shift for two years; my last years' service I shall come onto later. There was always much to do on shifts. We had 20 Britannias to play with, operating schedule services and other ad hoc commitments, flying troops and cargos worldwide. We also had other air forces pay us regular visits, together with many civilian Ministry of Defence chartered aircraft.

I can recall one of these operated by Monarch Airlines, a Bristol Britannia 312 series aircraft GAOVT, a reasonably frequent visitor. On one occasion it came in from its base at Luton airport for a cargo charter; it had a crew of three, one of whom had just been demobbed from RAF Lyneham. He was the aircraft's loadmaster. His old shift, of which he had been the corporal, was on duty. The flight sergeant in charge of the loaders never got on with this lad when he served there and the two of them clashed right away.

Incidentally this aircraft had come in without sufficient tie-down and lashing equipment. There was an almighty row over this, with this ex-corporal trying to flex his muscles within his new job, which of course had not the slightest effect on any of us, or indeed the flight sergeant. Eventually a consignment of the necessary lashing gear was loaned to this individual and he was made responsible for its safe keeping and return. All the cargo was eventually placed on the aircraft, leaving the bright new boy to see to it. As a result of this incident the powers that be contacted Monarch to let them know that in future this individual was persona non grata. We later heard that he was 'let go'.

On settling into our married quarter, we were told that it was going to be painted throughout. Up turned the painter chappie, who, as it happened, was one of the previous tenants of the house. He had got demobbed from the RAF and worked as a local painter and decorator. We had words with this guy, as he used up all our hot water for cleaning his brushes. Honest, I don't know how we managed to budget throughout each week, with my meagre wages.

Lita went into confinement in December 1968, and what a palaver it was trying to organize the transport to take her to the RAF Hospital at Wroughton. Later I was on shift and rang the hospital to find out how she was, to be told by the Princess Mary's Nursing Sister that she was just about to give birth. She kindly held the phone near to Lita and I heard all the screaming and shouting. Eventually I was told that we had a daughter, who we named Carol.

During our time at this married quarter, we had coal delivered to the house; we could only afford one sack per week, although it did not last the week through. On one occasion the coal merchant left us with a bag of coal dust. The next week Lita protested to the coalman, as we thought we were being done over. The following week, on looking to see if the coal shed contained a sack of decent coal bricks, we were surprised to find that we had been left with one very large lump of coal!

Lita got to know some of the other wives in this lonely outpost and she joined a football pools syndicate at a shilling a week. Just before she went to Spain to show off our new daughter to her parents, she won the very respectable sum of £79. This came at just the right time and was very gratefully received. On her return from Spain she bought a cylinder vacuum cleaner.

My time on shift at RAF Lyneham was fraught with hard physically and mentally-demanding work, especially the night shifts, as we had to load many aircraft for their early morning departures. All was not sweetness and light. Things had a habit of going wrong, with people letting one another down; individual grudges festered into outright hatred. At the same time friendships bloomed between those of a similar mind-set.

I recall that we had a sergeant in charge of our loading team of six, a Scotsman, who excelled in the consumption of his native malted fluids. He always wore an old best blue uniform, which seemed to have seen better days. He always turned up on time, looking to see what was what, and if the situation gave the opportunity, he would disappear for a topping–up session in the sergeants' mess.

Returning from one of these frequent missions, he was a bit the worse for wear and in a foul mood. This was further fuelled by the likes of me and others through a liberal amount of urine extraction. For some unknown reason he seemed, in his thin, erect unstable stature, to take offence. He then demanded the whereabouts of the section Land Rover, to, as he put it, inspect the work we had just toiled at. He disappeared off into a pea soup fog. Even if you were sober and the night time sky was a clear as a bell it was hard to navigate around the vastness of the aircraft parking area. We thought we would never see him again, hoping that he had wondered off into the depths of Wiltshire.

He suddenly reappeared in a frantic state, informing us that he had lost the Land Rover. It transpired that on leaving the safety of our vast hangar he had become lost and disoriented, and had got out of the vehicle to get his bearings (don't forget, it was very foggy). He had left the engine running, lights blazing, together with the flashing yellow light on top of the vehicle. He had then failed to relocate the Land Rover, but seeing through the haze the bright fuzzy lighting of our hangar, he had made a beeline for it, eventually getting back to the section.

He then told me to go find it and wandered off again into the haze – for a further topping-up, we presumed.

During the winter of 1969/70 the weather was really cold and often snowing, with icy conditions. Our section was located within a huge hangar where the freight was assembled for loading onto the aircraft. The powers that be decided that the flooring of the hanger needed digging up and relaying, so we were allocated another hangar. However it was over a mile away across the main road to Calne. Our offices and crew rooms stayed where they were. This situation further frustrated the already lengthy time and distance involved in collecting the freight and getting to the aircraft, which were sometimes at the far end of the aircraft parking area. Driving our specialist loading vehicles from our crew rooms to this hangar, then on towards the aircraft, gave us added problems, especially with the bad weather. Keeping warm and keeping the team and vehicles safe was the biggest concern.

The security within the military was heightened as a result of the hi-jacking's and bombings that were happening throughout Europe and the Middle East. Prior to this our airfield at Lyneham had been easily entered without too much trouble. This soon changed, with new fencing and security patrols by the RAF police. So much so, that we had to carry our identity documents whilst loading aircraft, for inspection by the RAF police. Just imagine the scene – working beneath a vehicle in the process of being lashed with chains, and being asked who you are and show your identity cards.

At the start of my last years' service, on a night shift, we had loaded three Hercules C130s aircraft; two flat floor loads and one palletized load, the latter being chained down and not using side guidance for securing. When we finished we were told to offload the palletized aircraft, and then rearrange the load to accommodate an urgently-needed aircraft propeller, required for an unserviceable aircraft up route, which was already loaded and secured onto a pallet. Two Condec loading vehicles were required to complete this task. Bear in mind that by this time it was early morning and we were all dog tired.

One was driven by me and the other by a tired, moaning, miserable git of a civilian driver. He had whined all night because he couldn't get any kip. Then to top it off we wanted his assistance again, at about 0700, when he was off duty at 0800, the same as us actually. He kept moaning throughout this exchange of pallets at the aircraft, pointing out, as loudly as he could, that he had a long way to go to collect his car from the MT section, together with the fact that he wouldn't get any overtime, so we had better hurry up, or he was off.

By now we had three pallets off onto one of the Condecs and the other one was at the aircraft, with the palletized propeller at the rear leaving room for the other pallets to come off the aircraft. Then we would turn the Condec around and load the propeller. An exchange of words ensued between me and the civilian driver, who quite frankly, by this time, I was really fed up with. This culminated in my suggesting that he should 'seek intercourse and depart', or words to that effect, thinking that he would just leave and walk away. But no, he jumped into the Condec at the aircraft, the one with the propeller on, slammed it into gear, reversed quickly, and braked hard to turn away from the aircraft. This had the effect of forcing the pallet with the propeller onto the rollered floor of the Condec, which had a chock to keep it in place from moving on the rollers. It overrode this chock and dropped with quite some force onto the concrete ground. Then he got out of the vehicle and disappeared.

It was nearly 0800, and all the camp were walking to work and had a splendid view of it all. I sat down on the edge of the aircraft ramp with my head in my hands, as if waiting for the handcuffs. I kept wondering through the tired haze what it would be like with a ball and chain round my ankles. Would the bread and water keep me sustained during my imprisonment? After all, they would have to blame someone, and I was in charge. What would happen to Lita in my absence? All sorts of other horrible things might come about as a result of this incident.

It wasn't long before I was brought up on a charge of 'not ensuring the security of a loaded Condec'. My name was entered on to a Charge Form, an RAF form 252. I was brought before the Squadron Wing Commander; I was dressed in my best uniform and marched in with two other corporals as escorts. Yep, I was on the carpet.

The charge was read out, and I was asked if I had anything to say. I said 'no sir'. He then went through my record of service, noting that I had an exemplary record. He then awarded me an Admonishment, which I suppose is a telling off.

The civilian driver who created the incident got off scot free. After all he was just the driver and I was in charge. Incidentally he avoided our section from then onwards. Whilst this was fine in itself, I just could not get over this incident. My whole attitude changed.

I was of a mind to do as many others had been doing for years – in other words, do as little as possible and keep out of sight.

The trouble was that the job I was doing on shift was very demanding; I had to get involved with the work in progress. So I asked for a transfer to the passenger section, which eventually came about. I then wrote a letter to the *Royal Air Force News*. At that time I think it was a monthly. I stated that I was employed within three trades, as a qualified supplier, a qualified Air Movements operative and a specialist vehicle driver. There was no other trade group that had this unpaid advantage over its airmen, or was there? If for instance I had taken the Supplier 1 Course, I would have been on a higher pay grade. There I was amongst others who were qualified in three trades. I felt it was wrong that this situation was not recognized by additional payment.

In writing this letter and having it published I must have stirred up a few of the powers that be, because shortly after I was informed that I was being posted to the stores at RAF St. Athan, 150 miles away in South Wales. I just could not believe it, but alas it was true. I immediately wrote a letter, which had to go through the proper channels, asking that this posting be cancelled: I only had nine months left to serve and I was serving my last tour of duty posting. Finally I kept asking myself, 'Why is this happening to me?' My morale at this point was even lower than before.

Finally I asked for a move away from the section to the Route Hotel, a site where departing families and others were accommodated overnight. It was wonderful; all I had to do was issue a few door keys. I spent most of my remaining time there wandering about and reading books and doing nothing really, except for writing letters to airlines and airports. With my mate Willkie we visited all the large airports on our days off, seeking out the people who mattered and getting ourselves known.

The chap in charge of the Route Hotel was a Master Air Load Master, (ALM = warrant officer) a nice guy, who like me was awaiting his time out for discharge. I don't know why, but I did not show this fellow the slightest bit of respect. Actually I cannot understand how he put up with me. At one point I felt sorry for him, because I would not have tolerated someone with an attitude like mine, if I was in his shoes. To be honest, I had this thing about ALMs.

I worked out that with a month's terminal leave, together with a month's annual leave and a month attached to a new employer, I could leave the RAF three months before my actual contract expired. So began a further intensive letter-writing campaign to many airlines and aviation companies.

One of the civilian airlines that came in for Ministry of Defence contracts was an airline called Lloyd International. They operated a fleet of two Britannia and two B707 aircraft in the passenger/freight role, and their base was at Stansted Airport. I wrote to their Flight Operations Manager seeking an interview and asking if I could spend some time with them to hone up on how things are done in Civvy Street.

I got a positive reply, and off I went for an interview. They agreed to my temporary attachment and some time later booked me a room in a local pub, so I got leave and off I went for two weeks. While I was there I was a bit disappointed at their unprofessional approach to working practices, and the scant knowledge of the employees to the safety and securing of cargoes. I was not impressed and thought better of committing myself to that company. A year later they went bust.

I had other interviews, one with Midland Air Cargo at Coventry Airport; I was interviewed by a lord. This airline operated Bristol Freighters, mostly carrying animals. They also went bust. I filled out an application for the Kenyan Air force, but they were only offering a three-year contract. I also went to Bournemouth Airport for an advertised vacancy in the Middle East with Air Work Services, but that too was a three-year contract.

I found that at that time there were plenty of opportunities for my future employment with companies in aviation. In fact it seemed my experience and qualifications were in great demand. By now I had a large file of job opportunities, although a former colleague of mine who chose an airline to work for at Heathrow had just been made redundant after a short period of employment. This made me think again about who I should be seeking to work for. There were other considerations to think about, such as settling down, owning property and raising a family in a stable environment.

So I then started looking for a job nearer to my parents' home in Bristol. I wrote to the airport at Lulsgate (Bristol Airport) and to Rolls Royce Operating, flying out of Filton. At that time Rolls Royce had a fleet of seven aircraft, including an Argosy, which I was very familiar with. This aircraft operated schedule services between Filton and Toulouse, France, in connection with the Concorde project. I attended both airfields for interviews, and surprisingly was offered jobs with both companies. The offer of a job with Rolls Royce, I was then told, would be put on hold, as the company had just gone into liquidation and no new posts could be taken up until the situation was clarified. Rolls Royce Operating was the last section of that large company to be settled and continue with its operations.

As the time for me to take up employment had reached the three-month period when I was allowed to leave the RAF, I chose the job offer at Bristol Airport, and started work there on 1st June 1971.

# CHAPTER 8

# CIVVY STREET

As part of the demob process, I was offered an interview with one of the officials at the Department of Employment in the centre of Bristol. I duly arrived for this meeting in a suit, all spick and span as I reported to reception. This is one of those times that really stick out in my travels through life. Inside a large hall were a large number of men and women, all pushing, shouting and swearing to get near to the reinforced glass partitions, where sat several ladies asking questions of those who had made it to the front.

This was a real eye-opener for me as I had never witnessed this sort of behaviour before, although I had been warned many times that Civvy Street was not the RAF. Eventually, as I had an appointment, I was seen by a chap in an office. It turned out to be an informal chat, during which he advised me to sign on in the RAF. It was a bit late for that! All he wanted to do was gossip about his time in Bomber Command. I came out of there perplexed, and wondered if I was doing the right thing. What a waste of time and effort in getting there.

I also made contact with a retired wing commander who was the Forces Retirement Liaison Officer; he had an office in Bristol, where I met him. He gave me lots of advice about settling down into civilian life, and he too suggested that I seek to sign on. He did give me some much-needed advice on getting a mortgage, and gave me the assurance that he was available to assist with the settling-in process during the transition from service life to becoming a civilian.

I don't know how others managed their departure from the RAF, but I was getting rather nervous about the whole thing. My dad had given me the 'evil eye' over my leaving as well. After all I was 30 years old, I had spent half my life in the RAF, I knew nothing about civilian life and I was very apprehensive of the future prospects that awaited me. All this made me aware that I must succeed in my new chosen career. I accepted the challenge and prepared myself for the unknown to come.

Before finally leaving RAF Lyneham for pastures new I sought out one of our officers, our Duty Air Movements Officer (DAMO). He had interviewed me after the propeller incident and told me that he was saddened that I wanted to move away from his shift. He was very kind and expressed his gratitude at my efforts in training new lads to the job and for moulding the team into a professional unit of skilled air movers.

I took the opportunity to ask him for a reference for my future employment interviews, which he said he would post to me from his new appointment in Washington. I eventually received it.

On leaving the RAF after a total of 15 years boy and man, I was not entitled to a pension, because at that time you had to complete 22 years' adult service. Now, as I understand it, you only have to complete two years' military service to entitle you to a deferred pension. This does not of course apply to those of us who saw service before these rules came into being in 1975. There has of course been an attempt to seek redress to this anomaly, unfortunately without success. Naturally I feel this shows a blatant disregard for all us servicemen who served their country with distinction. One wonders how this cannot be changed.

## Bristol Airport

I started work at Bristol Airport on the 1ˢᵗ June 1971. At that time the airport was owned by the City of Bristol, so I became a corporation employee.

This airport has an interesting history. It was initially going to be called RAF Broadfield Down, but was changed to RAF Lulsgate Bottom. Work started on laying down the runway on the 11ᵗʰ June 1941 and the completed airfield was declared operational on the 15ᵗʰ of January 1942. Flying actually started before the Wimpy bulldozers had finished laying down the 3891 foot (1186 meters) east-west main runway. With all the buildings it cost £309,000 in 1941.

On the misty morning of 24ᵗʰ July 1941 at 0610 hours, the wartime workers had just started work when out of the blue, to their astonishment, an aircraft landed on the unfinished runway and came to a halt nearby. One of the construction gang, an Irish fellow, recognized that it wasn't an RAF plane, but a German one. He quickly realized that he had better do something and drove his tractor in front of the now stationary aircraft, a twin-engine Luftwaffe JU88 A4 bomber of 3/KG 30. He shouted to his mates to 'call out the guard,' or words to that effect. The four crew got out of the plane and the pilot asked the startled Emerald Isle worker, in French, 'What part of France is this?' As he did not understand the reply, he realized that something was amiss, drew his pistol and made haste back towards the aircraft, shouting instructions to his crew. They did not get far as they were hemmed in by the tractor.

Shortly after this the military arrived and after a lot of shouting and waving of (possibly unloaded) rifles, the soldiers persuaded the invaders to surrender. These German chaps had been on a bombing mission from their base at Lanveoc-Poulmic in France, where they had taken off at 2335 hours on 23rd July 1941 to bomb the Birkenhead Docks. On their way back they had become disorientated due to the RAF radiating electronic countermeasures from Lympsham, south east of Weston-Super-Mare in Somerset, onto their homing beacon at Brest. They had mistaken the Welsh coast for Cornwall, having crossed the Bristol Channel, which they thought was the English Channel, and as they were getting very low on fuel, they landed on the first airfield they saw, which they thought was in France.

This aircraft was indeed a prize. Captured intact and fully flyable, it was first flown to the Royal Aircraft Establishment (RAE) at Farnborough, for evaluation, then onto RAF Collywestern to join 1426 Enemy Aircraft Flight, known as 'RAFWAFFE'. The aircraft was painted in RAF colours, given the registration number of EE205 and joined the many other captured AXIS aircraft and used for a variety of purposes.

The German aircrew were Uffz. (Corporal) Wolfgang Hosie (F) Pilot; Fw. (Sergeant) Paul Zimmermann (B) Observer/Navigator/Bomb aimer; Ogefr. (Leading Aircraftsman) Franz Sander (Bf) Wireless Operator; and Ogefr. (Leading Aircraftsman) Robert Riemann (Bs) Gunner. Under interrogation, they were not very communicative, although admitting to their navigational errors. They spent the rest of the war as prisoners of war.

History or not, I did wonder if I had made the right decision in going to Bristol Airport. Would I fit in? Was this the right choice for a career? Well, it's too late now buddy, I said to myself. I was employed as a member of the duty crew as a fireman and airfield labourer. Among the duties was baggage and cargo handling, and they even had one of those large forklifts.

One of my tasks was to put out 'goosenecks', paraffin-filled containers similar to watering cans with a wick coming out of the spout. We had to place these either side of the small runway in crosswind conditions for small aircraft as the runway lighting when the daylight was fading.

During my interview, the Airport Director told me that he was shortly going to introduce the post of Airport Duty Officer. He was awaiting the approval of the Airport Committee before going ahead with the advertising. He suggested that I would make a suitable candidate, but told me to keep my mouth shut about it. I was to be paid weekly and on getting my first pay slip, I was astounded to read that my employee number was the same as the last three digits of my RAF number, 824. Wow! I took this to be a good sign.

It was a further nine months before the interviews started and I got one of the jobs. There were five of us; an ex RAF apprentice (Similar to myself, although I was an Boy Entrant), Sqn/Ldr Harry Pollard (my old boss) and two other ex RAF bods, one of whom was a Chinese linguist, the other an ex RAF armourer, who had also been previously employed on the Duty Crew, like me.

I must admit that those first nine months were something of a challenge. I was thrust amongst several family members who had populated the whole workforce for many years without change; I soon learnt that it was unwise to proffer suggestions for improvements or changing working practices. I really felt ostracized and it was like being a foreigner amongst a collection of 18<sup>th</sup> century West Country farmers.

Setting up a new department in an organization that had a mind-set from the Stone Age was extremely difficult and led to much animosity, distrust and bloody-mindedness against us. These were extremely difficult times for me and my colleagues. The biggest problem we had to face was the Union. If you don't happen to know how unions work, this is a system whereby if you ask a member of the workforce to do a specific task and they don't like it, it's classed as either bullying or 'not my job mate'. Things did not improve when we were kitted out with our new tailored uniforms; this became a source of amusement and continual cat-calling and mutterings of 'anyone call for a taxi' or 'your chauffeur is here mate.' This went on for years.

The fire section and Air Traffic Control are the only two sections that can close an airport by withdrawing their labour. The number and types of fire vehicles and their manning is laid down as part of the airfield licence; boy did the fire section take advantage of that fact. They worked a wonderful scam with overtime. There was minimal manning required to operate the fire vehicles and this was worked to full advantage, mostly with sickness cover.

In those early days the total airport authority workforce was about 100, while the airlines and all other employees I estimated to be less than 1000. In those early days the security of the airfield boundaries was not all it should have been. One fine Sunday, Air Traffic Control called the fire section to ask one of them to intercept a car that was driving down the main runway. It was duly stopped, checked and escorted to safety. The occupants were a priest and two nuns who had somehow got lost on the airport; the priest did say that he had never been on a road that wide before.

The airport underwent many different growing pains. The

aircraft movements went up and down with the recessions and the various fuel crises that we all had to endure. Then during August 1972 Lita and I were blessed with another beautiful daughter, who we named Carmen.,

The difference between my life as an RAF Air Movements corporal and my new career were miles apart. For a start I was involved in making decisions of policy and manning requirements, including recruitment, and I attended management meetings regarding anything to do with the general running of the airport. For my various individual responsibilities I had a budget to adhere to.

One incident that comes to mind from those very early days happened at about 0650 one wintry morning when I arrived at work to open up the terminal building (our hours of operation at the time were 0700 to 2200 daily) to find that the doors were locked. I was surrounded by quite a few other people who wanted to get inside out of the cold. I could see our night watchman lying on a sofa at the far end of the building, apparently fast asleep. I and several others banged and shouted for some time before he came to his senses. Remember there were no mobile phones in those days.

As aircraft numbers and passenger figures increased, the running of the airport was constantly being reviewed with staffing levels and job descriptions, sometimes with the cooperation of those concerned and sometimes not. It soon became apparent that any changes to the job descriptions as previously agreed would lead to a regrading request and then an appeal if it failed the first time. I count myself amongst those who went down this path, which I was successful in negotiating quite a few times.

During my 27 years to the day (1st June 1971 to 1st June 1998) I witnessed many changes to my working conditions and to the airport's rise in passenger throughput from 100,000 to 1 million (nowadays I understand that it's more like 6 million). Stress levels at times were very prevalent within the management, with several section heads and others suffering nervous breakdowns; there were two section heads who died, independently of each other after getting home from work. Others went off sick and we never saw them again.

In those early days we seemed to be constantly increasing the passenger figures, but it was a very slow process under local authority authorship to get anything done to alleviate the situation. An anti-airport group of local residents was formed which seemed to oppose every planning application, causing delays to any new building projects. I understand that this is still the situation today.

There were of course some interesting visitors. I was asked to be the liaison officer between the airport and the Goodyear airship Europa which came to visit us. This beautiful 'blimp' stayed with us for about a fortnight. The airship came on a goodwill visit as a thank you to local garages and tyre distributors who had met certain sales targets. They were then invited as guests for a trip around the skies of Bristol. At the time the airship was based in Italy and all the crew were Italians.

My job was to coordinate the passengers as they arrived and allocate the seating arrangements within the gondola; there were six seats. I also recorded the passenger details in a manifest book. I must admit that I checked out the co-pilot's seat on several trips.

I had to man the phone during their stay, and used to get all sorts of enquires. These would be not only from the press and other media interests demanding seats but the general public as well. There were the usual complainers who wanted it to go away or be shot down, as well as the many people who wanted a free ride or even to pay for one, which Goodyear was not allowed to do.

One lady, phoning on behalf of her elderly mother, would not take no for an answer. She constantly kept phoning and pleading for her mother to have a flight. The Goodyear boss said 'no, stop asking me'. The media soon got hold of the story, and I eventually fitted her in for a flight.

The stories of my 27 years at Bristol International Airport are my own personal accounts of how I saw events and situations. In no way must they be interpreted as an official account of the airport authority, individuals or the airlines mentioned.

Aviation can be a fickle business. It's amazing when I look back to my early days in civil aviation the number of airlines that seemed to come and go. When they start off operating schedules or holiday flights, the airline management are keen to exercise their power of generating business. Which is fine in itself, but coping with their insatiable demands can be very trying. I recall that some of these seemed to have the impression that the airport came under their jurisdiction, which could make some of the airline management somewhat difficult to deal with.

In the early 1970s Court Line commenced holiday flights from Bristol with their multi-coloured BAC1-11s to Mediterranean destinations. They operated nine BAC1-11 500 series aircraft, together with other larger aircraft, from their base at Luton. Not all the 1-11s operated from Bristol at the same time. They gave them all individual names, i.e. 'Halcyon Cloud'- 'Halcyon Sky' etc.

This was a time of expansion of 'package tours' in conjunction with Clarkson's Holidays. A whole new way of taking holidays was being established for the British public. For us in Terminal management, a whole new set of problems emerged as a result of the increased throughput of passengers, and our terminal building was, at times, bursting at the seams.

With this new airline, came an awakening for us sedentary West

Country plodders to the antics and working methods of these Luton-based personnel. All of a sudden we became aware that we had in our midst a large collection of 'batters for the other side', of both sexes, bringing with them a wonderful insight into the life of the London-based airline staff. Meeting some of the male check-in staff and cabin crew who came to us on temporary secondment from Luton to set up their operation at Bristol was an eye opener. It was new for us to see so many males wearing make-up!

A recruiting drive for locally-based cabin crew commenced. Hundreds applied, which were soon whittled down to the required numbers. Those that could not swim, open the aircraft doors or had inadequate knowledge of first aid stood no chance.

I remember one day coming across (possibly the wrong word) one of the hostesses, who was crying her eyes out. She was hysterical. It transpired that she had come in for her pay, but none was forthcoming for that month. In fact she had received an enormous bill from the airline. She had been charged, as the senior cabin crew member, for an amount of unaccountable missing duty free goods from the flights she had been on. She had no idea how her share of the rent and other necessary expenditure, for the coming weeks ahead would be met. Her pleas of innocence to her management were not met with any sympathy or tolerance.

What was happening? What had gone wrong? The police were called and a thorough, secretive, investigation unfolded an amazing series of events. To save time and money, the airline had negotiated a deal with the duty-free bonded warehouse whereby, for each flight, two sets of containers sealed by HM Customs would be loaded onto the aircraft, here at Bristol. The seals could not be broken until clear of UK airspace, which incidentally did not give the cabin crew a lot of time to check the contents against the lists. The second set of containers was stowed in the hold. The aircraft on landing overseas had quick turnarounds, and by the time all the passengers and their baggage had been offloaded and re-loaded, together with the containers being swapped round, all the time had gone. The same thing happened here at Bristol. Some aircraft had three or more flights a day.

It came to light that more than a handful of customs officers, along with the bonded warehouse manager, were short-filling the containers and sharing the spoils. There was a court case, the warehouse manager finished up in jail and there was a huge shake-up in HM Customs and lots of new faces.

Some of the Court Line crews at the end of the day's flights used to hold parties on board their aircraft. This used to infuriate the aircraft cleaners, who had a time limit to clean each aircraft. These parties used to last for ages, during which, I understand, training and instruction for both sexes for the various stages of the Mile High Club, may have been undertaken.

You may remember that Court Line purchased the last remaining airworthy ex-RAF Beverley XB259. It was flown to Luton. Their intention was to use this aircraft for ferrying L1011 Tri-Star Rolls Royce RB 211 engines. Unfortunately they could not get the civilian airworthiness certificate. At that time they were experiencing financial difficulties.

The airline went into liquidation on August 15th 1974. The Beverley was sold to the military museum at Fort Paull, east of Hull, where it remains on display as the sole survivor of this type.

Unfortunately, I had gone with Court Line to our home in Spain in August 1974, when they went bust, and got stuck at Santiago de Compostela. I had to borrow the money to get back home!

CHAPTER 9

# PARAMOUNT AIRWAYS

Paramount operated two MD 83 aircraft out of Bristol Airport between 1987 and 1990. They also had aircraft based at other airports. The Bristol Airport Managing Director would go out of his way to negotiate special financial deals to either attract or keep airlines based with us here at Bristol. This airline was the first to instigate a no-smoking policy.

We were understandably over the moon at getting an airline based with us. Special arrangements with accommodation, landing, aircraft parking, and many other concessions were made to complete the deal. This was much to the annoyance of other operators, but as the MD pointed out to them, 'give us the same amount of passenger throughput and deals will be made!'

These deals were supposed to be confidential commercial undertakings, but somehow word would get out about their special concessions, much to the annoyance of agents and other operators. Civil aviation is a cut-throat business.

Over the previous years different airlines had come and departed, mostly going bust. So this was a prize for us and meant that our passenger figures would rise together with our profits. I should point out that at this time, there was very little to offer at Bristol. There were, and still are, no large hangars. Also at that time our fuel holding capacity was very limited, together with no Instrument Landing System (ILS) and only 6600 feet of runway to play with. Aircraft parking was also limited. Trying to provide additional new accommodation, or indeed any sort of change to the planned layout of the infrastructure, was time consuming and subject to local opposition and the dreaded planning applications. This, I understand, is still the situation today.

The special deal for Paramount used to infuriate us in Terminal Management, because as the passenger numbers increased, we had to try and give some sort of guidance in the use of our limited passenger facilities. The departure lounge was on many occasions bursting at the seams and there wasn't enough car parking. The handling agencies and Paramount would not adhere to agreed procedures for calling passengers to the lounge, totally ignoring our requests and only being concerned about their own aircraft turnarounds.

This of course caused many passenger complaints, either in writing or in person, which I and my colleagues had to deal with. We instigated a customer complaint form, which created much letter writing. All letters had to be answered by whoever was on shift at the time. These letters, and there were lots, took up most of the time on night shifts. Nights were busy enough as it was.

Regular meetings were arranged to sort out all these problems, minutes taken and procedures updated and agreed, but alas we were totally ignored. Animosity and hatred ensued between different individuals of different companies.

It all came to a head one day when the MD of Paramount Airways was informed by his fellow directors at a board meeting, that he had, as a result of his unorthodox management style, been voted off the board. This gentleman was a bit miffed about all this, as he had put £11.5 million of his own money into forming the airline. As a result, he worked a flanker with the company accounts, transferring all his cash back into his personal account. He then promptly disappeared off the scene to somewhere in the United States, leaving the airline bankrupt. His Rolls Royce was later found abandoned in the car park at Dublin Airport. All their staff were quite unceremoniously left overnight without a job, causing much heartbreak and upset. Not to mention all the passengers throughout Europe who were stranded. The airport was of course many millions out of pocket as a result. Liens were placed on the aircraft at Bristol until a satisfactory agreement was reached with the aircraft's owners.

Eventually after about two years this man re-entered the country and was arrested and duly sentenced for this selfish undertaking.

I write this account of the demise of this airline to show you the fickleness of some of those in high positions, who have vast amounts of cash, but suffer from vainness and pure greed.

Just as an afterthought…

During the checking in of one of their flights the concourse was full of people, and all the check-in desks had queues reaching to the main doors. One of the check-in staff left her post to bring a rather angry lady to my office. She was beside herself with rage, and I was the one to receive the full blast. She complained that the airport bus from Bristol to the airport had driven past her without stopping whilst she was at the proper bus stop, and she had to fork out for a taxi. She demanded the £12 from me. The bus company, by the way, was First Bus. Nothing I could think of to say would pacify her rage.

Then from the corner of my eye I noticed the bus pull in outside the terminal. I told the lady that I would sort this out with the bus driver and get back to her. I spoke to the driver, who said there had been no one at the bus stop when he passed. He then offered to speak to the lady.

What transpired next was a classic. We found her in the checking-in queue. He said to her, 'Where were you at the bus stop?' She said she was sheltering from the rain on the steps of Debenhams, At which he shouted at the top of his voice that he did not drive his bus up the steps of f★★★★g Debenhams. She went as red as beetroot. Before walking away I suggested to the lady that if she wanted to apologize to me I would be in my office. Of course I never saw her again.

If you thought the problems with Paramount Airways were an isolated incident, then think on. There were many others. I remember when the Managing Director tried really hard to initiate a transatlantic holiday service to Miami. A deal was finally arranged with an American airline which operated a rather old Boeing 707. They could not operate with a full passenger load into and out of Bristol Airport, due to insufficient runway length. Nevertheless a flight schedule was arranged to operate to and from the States via a refuelling stop at Prestwick Airport, in Scotland.

The MD and all of us were delighted; the local media were all in attendance for the inaugural flight. Word arrived that the B707 had landed at Prestwick - but there was a problem. The aircraft captain had radioed to Prestwick that he required refuelling on arrival. The refuelling bowser driver arrived at the aircraft, and asked the captain how he would like to pay. It transpired that the crew had not got a recognized refuelling carnet, or indeed any cash. The captain asked that the airline be billed. He was told that their airline was not an approved customer and unless some form of recognized payment method was provided, they would not get any fuel. So the bowser driver drove off. The handling agency had also got wind of this and also demanded up-front cash payment. As this was not forthcoming there was an almighty problem, with lots of phone calls between Bristol, Prestwick and the States.

Well our MD went ballistic. It was finally resolved, after a three-hour delay, when he offered to act as guarantor. Those poor passengers who were at Bristol and Prestwick not being aware of this financial upset on landing at Bristol, the press had mostly gone, so an opportunity to gain some much-needed publicity had vanished. The publicity that this story would have generated if the real reason for the aircraft's delay had got out would not have been welcome. It should have been sorted by the American airline beforehand. It just goes to show how poorly organized some of these lesser known airlines were in those days of long ago.

There was of course a further problem at Bristol regarding payment for fuel. Because of these delays passengers had to receive food vouchers, further escalating the 'who's going to pay?' problem. The agent at Bristol had also been in touch with their sister company at Prestwick, escalating a problem which already seemed insurmountable.

There was supposed to be a regular summer weekly flight, but only three of these took place and they were all delayed, through a variety of problems. Would it surprised you to know that this airline soon disappeared into the great unknown and went bust? A lot of revenue had to be written off and many disgruntled passengers, both here and in the States, had to make alternative arrangements.

We had another airline called Air Bristol. They started operations in 1982 with two De Havilland Doves and a DH Heron. They had a ground staff of three girls and a station manager who operated from a tiny office in the terminal. They managed to get approval to operate services between Bristol and Leeds/Bradford together with ad hoc charters.

On the very first flight out of Bristol the passenger load consisted of the Bristol Lord Mayor and other dignitaries, including our MD, all on a return trip. They were being met by senior dignitaries of Leeds/Bradford. Would you believe it, on landing at Leeds/Bradford the captain of the Dove had no cash and no fuel carnet. As you can imagine there were a lot of phone calls to try and sort it out. The chief pilot of Air Bristol was at Bristol, on the receiving end of the calls. For some reason the senior management of the airline were not contactable on the golf course (remember, no mobiles in those days).

It was agreed that the chief pilot would hand to me a company cheque for the outstanding amounts for landing, handling and fuel. On receipt of this cheque, I was then to phone our MD to say it was in my hand. When I went to find this chief pilot he saw me and ran off, giving me some excuse that he was in a hurry and would get back to me.

I never did get that cheque. It transpired that the chief pilot was not authorized to sign company cheques. Furthermore he had not even got a company cheque book. Once more an arrangement was made with our airport and the flight with its dignitaries flew back to Bristol.

The airline had a further problem before disappearing into the history books. One of the Doves developed an engine snag. The company was surprised at this, as on purchasing the aircraft they had been assured that the engines had received a full overhaul. It transpired that one of the engines had been fitted with the wrong size pistons. It made a lovely sound though. Oh, and the three girls that were employed all walked out, as they could not stand the aggressive manner of their station manager. Apparently he thought he was God. Shortly after this, the airline went bust. I seem to be mentioning a lot of airlines that went bust, but it's a fact of life within civil aviation.

I had a phone call from Dublin one fine morning, from someone in Aer Turas operations (they operated from 1962 to 2003). He wanted to know if they could get a discount for operating their CL44 EI-BGO into Bristol for a one off charter. They used to come in with horses for the Cheltenham Gold Cup races, a once a year visit. This also generated other charter aircraft, carrying hundreds of passengers from the Emerald Isle.

I checked with our accounts department. Their answer was no, and could I ask Aer Turas to please pay for last year's visit, together with an agreed method of payment for this trip! The airline's reply was that they would fly into Cardiff. I told them I had already phoned Cardiff to warn them. They too were owed money by this airline.

The passengers of various airlines for these flights were an almighty handful. By the time they reached us for departure back to Dublin/Cork, the vast majority were three sheets to the wind and it was an almighty task to get them to board their respective aircraft. The cleaning of the terminal building, when they had gone, especially the toilets, took some organizing, and much complaining from our cleaners.

Every day there was some catastrophic incident to rectify. I recall that one time in the checking-in concourse, there was lots of shouting and passengers making complaints to the information desk. I got the brunt of all these furious people. It transpired that whilst the checking in was proceeding along nicely for the 130 passengers on a holiday flight, the checking-in assistant had left his desk to help a pregnant lady, travelling on her own with three toddlers. He put her cases onto the scales. After dealing with her he moved onto the next person in line, who happened to be an aggressive, booze-fuelled local publican. He was asked to place his baggage onto the scales, at which he flew into a torrential rage of swearing and abuse and demanded that the assistant load them for him, as he had done for the pregnant lady.

The assistant's explanation to this gent stood no chance of being understood. This became too much for the checking–in lad to handle and he promptly left his desk and went home. All hell broke loose, as for quite a while there was no one available to replace this lad. This situation further escalated, as there was a tight schedule for the aircraft turnaround, and possibly a loss of the aircraft slot time.

Some of the passengers were furious with this landlord chap and there were blows exchanged between some of both the ladies and gents who were standing in line. At the same time lots of other flights were checking in. The concourse was full to bursting.

I was asked by one of the cleaners one day if it was all right for her to borrow one of our industrial vacuum cleaners for use by the taxi office. I was often asked by various tenants in the terminal if they could borrow things. I asked her to tell this chap to come and see me, as I was not going to lend one out for use in cleaning their cars. He came and assured me that it was for cleaning their little counter office. I made sure that one was available and gave him instructions that it was not to be returned without being emptied.

About half hour later, as it was quiet in the arrivals concourse, I thought this machine had been gone for rather a long time, so I went round to see what was up. I caught five taxi drivers in the process of sucking out toys from a vending machine, using our vacuum. The machine was one of those that had a sort of crane, where you put money in and tried to manoeuvre it to pick up a cuddly toy. It seemed they all wanted one for their beloveds, as

Christmas was not far off. They were made to pay for them, but goodness knows how many had gone beforehand.

On a night shift I was having a bit of a problem with one of the cleaners, who had not been with us for more than a few months. I sought him out and told him that I wanted a certain area cleaned straight away, as shortly the area would be filled with passengers. He told me that he was busy and walked away mumbling.

I was not going to stand for that. I called him back and asked him to meet me in my office 'now!' He got himself really worked up at this and swore and gestured, saying 'Who the bloody hell do you think you are?' He threw his ID card on my desk and told me to 'stick your job up your arse,' then departed from the airport.

I wrote a report out for the HR director and told him that I did not want this individual back. I also asked if he could foresee any repercussions from this incident. The next day the cleaner turned up full of apologies and said he would get back to work. But I told him I had accepted his resignation and that he was no longer an employee. If he wanted any due pay, he was to return all his clothing in a clean and tidy condition. Incidentally, it's far easier if someone resigns than it is to sack them, as it always seems to go to arbitration, costing a lot of time and money.

I would just like to mention three of the people I worked closely with. Firstly my immediate boss, who was on the receiving end of the MD's target practice. It got to the stage where he just could not come into work. He was hounded at every shift and presented with demanding tasks on top of the daily routine. After the usual period of sickness he was made redundant and his job reorganized. I was his best man at his wedding. On leaving the airport he packed up and moved to France, where he now teaches English.

Then a colleague of mine I worked closely with went off sick, as he seemed to have constant diarrhoea. He underwent a series of tests, which culminated in him having an exploratory operation to find out what the problem was. He was opened up and they found he was at an advance stage of stomach/intestinal cancer. He was closed up and informed that he had a life expectancy of six more weeks.

Prior to this he had been having a fling with one of the information desk ladies. They were of course both married to other partners; they had been living together for a few months when this news about his illness came about. He had been married for more than 25 years and had six grown-up offspring. Eventually his wife agreed to a divorce, which was hastily arranged, and a marriage to his new lady was performed. This of course would mean that the ex-wife would lose her entitlement to his pension and death benefits. The ceremony took place in the flat where they lived, as he was too ill to make it to the church, even though it was just around the corner. I was a witness and read an appropriate prayer. It was a heart-wrenching ceremony. He actually kept going for 12 more weeks before he finally received the call.

His replacement was recruited from Luton Airport. He had been made redundant from his senior position there, with many others, when Court Line went bust. He was a lovely guy. He was placed in tandem with my shifts for his first month to learn the local procedures. He had previously worked alongside our MD when they had both been at Luton. We got on well and spent time together when off duty.

He had been with us for about six months when he pulled me to one side and told me he had been head-hunted by the new owners of Liverpool Airport. He was offered all sorts of concessions to take the post of Operations Director, including a car, all his removal expenses and a share in the company bonus scheme, so off he went.

I met him about 18 months later when he came to visit me and others at work. He said he had settled in nicely to his new position, having made many changes to their existing operational procedures. He told me that one morning just before leaving home he had got a call from one of the directors asking to meet him in a motorway services. When he got there he was asked for his car keys and ID card, and told that he had been made redundant. He was also asked what he wanted from his office, as he was not permitted to return. He was given a generous pay off. They had a taxi waiting to take him home. Beware of strangers offering gifts!

I have made reference to our Managing Director; He came to us in 1980 from Luton, where he had been the Commercial Director. He bought a house at the side of the airfield, and was constantly chasing section heads up. It seemed he never went home. Every morning, or even at night time, he wandered around with his 'little black book' jotting down things to chase individuals up about at the next morning's management meeting. He even on occasion demanded meetings at night, if there had been an incident or something of a serious nature affecting airfield operations, and expected every section head to come in.

The morning management meetings were referred to as 'morning prayers'. All section heads had to give a verbal report of the operations within their sections of the last 24 hours. Everyone, without exception, feared these morning prayer meetings. After listening to each individual in turn, he would dish out orders that they were to follow before the next meeting. When all had said their piece, out would come the little black book and without fail he would pick on one or more section heads and chastise them in front of all present, very often telling them to stay behind, when he would lose his temper and lay into them, not for short periods but for at least an hour. He was a past master at interrogation.

He had a Jekyll and Hyde personality, as with the media, councillors, tenants, agents and airline chiefs, he was a brilliant negotiator. The treatment of his subordinates was something different. There were those amongst us who had nervous breakdowns.

His relationship with the local TV and radio stations was legendary. He was constantly seeking to promote his airport, so much so that he instigated for me and my colleagues to make three morning broadcasts and one at 1700 hrs every day on Radio Bristol, giving news of delays and other interesting goings on at the airport. That was fine in itself, although he listened to most of them and was critical of each individual's on-air performance. I personally used to shake with fear on doing these broadcasts, knowing that he would be listening and that shortly after the 0700 transmission he would phone in and be critical, or demand reasons for delays or ask questions about the weather or other operational stuff. It was doubly frustrating as he knew the answers to the questions he was asking. A lot of these questions were brought about by various individuals who had phoned him and told him what was happening. Yes, by back-stabbing bastards! You could just not escape his demands. He even used to phone for updates twice a day or even more, dependent on operational requirements from the many trips he made abroad for conferences and contract negotiations. He was in Amsterdam on one occasion when another airport director, who was in the next hotel room to him, was murdered by the 'rent boy' he had picked up.

After one of the 0700 broadcasts I was making, I sat there waiting for his call, knowing he would have a barrage of questions that he wanted answers to. He was driving to work and his car had a car phone installed. Unfortunately he crashed his car and died as a result.

I have missed out an awful lot of his treatment of some of the individuals who bore the brunt of his aggressive management style. Even those in the Council who had dealings with the airport feared his wrath. Just before his death he was awarded an OBE for his services to aviation. His predecessor had also departed as the result of a car crash.

In those early days, airport security was becoming an issue with the new Government legislation, especially in relation to cars being left unattended in front of terminal buildings. All we could do to enforce this legislation was use the Tannoy system to try and locate the offenders and get them to remove their vehicles. Car park charges at airports are expensive and it would seem that visitors to the airport would chance their luck at getting away without having to pay. One day, over a reasonably quiet weekend whilst I was on duty, the MD called me and told me to get rid of a car which had been left abandoned at the terminal entrance. I informed him that I had already put out several announcements, but no one had come forward.

He lost it at this, ranting at me to get rid of it. I again put out further announcements, but no one came forward. He bleeped me again and again and got progressively angrier, I knew what was coming, and sure enough he laid into me to sort it out. This resulted in both of us shouting our heads of at each other. He accused me of making him have a nervous breakdown. My suggestion to him was that he was the one giving me a nervous breakdown! I had no equipment or manpower at my disposal to move the car.

He was in his secretary's office overlooking the front of the terminal building whilst all this was going on, and with him was his secretary and her husband; she had been called on this Saturday to do some work. All his shouting and the many calls to me were witnessed by these two. This situation really got to me, and by now I was in turmoil, as I knew he would not forget this incident and there would be repercussions to follow.

A few minutes later his secretary and her husband departed through the main entrance, got into the offending car and were about to drive off. I stopped them and asked if they were aware that they had been responsible for all this upset with the MD. She just said 'sorry, Gerry'. I looked up towards the window of her office and saw the MD looking at us. It transpired that he knew perfectly well whose car it was, but would not say anything to his secretary or her husband. I got on the phone to him, and another shouting match took place. He was not going to admit that he knew all this. His response was that no matter whose car it was, I should have got it removed.

This incident – and there were many similar ones over the years – had a nerve-racking effect on me, and others also had to endure similar experiences with him.

I had many responsibilities and duties to perform, one of which was to keep an eye on contractors, especially builders. Eventually a contracts liaison manager was employed, as we were not satisfied with some of the standard of work on completion. Two other senior positions were also created to administer and organize the building regulations and local planning applications. There were some big named companies involved at various times, with the continual expansion of our facilities. They would get the contract and immediately sub-contract the work to smaller firms who were supposed to be specialists in their fields.

These contractors would arrive on site, do their bit and disappear. We would then go to the main contracts liaison chappie and tell him the job had not been carried out to the specification required. My, did this cause some almighty rows.

Just to give a few examples; an expansion of the aircraft parking area was completed. The contract stated that the materials used must be of a certain depth, throughout the entire area. By using special circular depth-digging drills, core samples would be extracted at intervals throughout the area covered. This was always clearly stated within the contract specifications. It cost the main contractors dearly to put things right.

On one occasion, new windows were fitted airside on the first floor restaurant facing the aircraft parking area. We noticed that there were rather large gaps at either end before the gaps were covered up. It was obvious that the measurements were short, and for us this meant that these windows, when receiving jet blast, would probably cave in. This was of course eventually put right. As a result of the airport's supervision of contractors' standards, word soon got around that jobs had to be done properly.

One final incident worth mentioning. A new departure lounge extension was opened, by Princess Anne. During the first weekend of using these new facilities, because of the amount of passenger throughput, the new toilets soon became flooded and effluent flooded into the lounge. The smell was terrible and it caused the Airport quite some embarrassment. Eventually the contractor was found and his presence demanded at the airport. He soon found the problem, after opening one of the outside manhole covers. The builders had placed some used cement bags into the pipes so as (we were informed) to stop rats getting into the system before they were commissioned. They had been left in place, causing a backwash of the sewage.

I might add that not many of these contractors received the full amount of the contracted price, some not receiving anything. They were told to sue if they wished; none did, as far as I know.

# CHAPTER 10

# ADVENTURES AT
# BRISTOL AIRPORT

In the late 1980s Bristol Airport was getting busier, with aircraft movements and passenger throughput at such a level that 24-hour operation was now the norm.

Airports had become very sensitive to the world-wide threats from terrorism; it therefore became necessary to restructure the security section. The incidences of bombings and hi-jacking's together with new Government legislation, had made this a priority. This had up to now been the responsibility of us in terminal management.

Therefore a new post of Chief Security Officer was created. Interviews took place and an ex-RAF flight lieutenant was recruited, quite a nice chap. He had been with us for a short while when he popped into my office to say goodbye. I said, 'where you off to then?' He said, 'I've had enough and I am off. I've been told to wear a uniform, and I am not doing that for anyone!'

So that was that. Another set of interviews took place and an ex-RAF warrant officer policeman was recruited. He wore a uniform similar to a police inspector.

After a couple of years, it was decided to carry out another review of the Security Section. The review recommended appointing a Senior Airport Security Manager and five duty security officers, together with the guards we already had. The Chief Security Officer was invited to apply for one of the posts, or take redundancy. He chose the latter. I wonder why?

The other five posts were recruited from ex-forces SNCOs, Army, Navy and RAF. Over time they all left. One died. Three were dismissed, at different times for different reasons, and one immigrated to the USA to become a Red Indian chieftain... I daren't say any more, but if we ever meet, I would amaze you with the details!

This section, as with others, was to be reviewed several more times as the airport got progressively busier. As with any business it's the employees that we all come into contact with. It's rather different at airports as there are many different companies that have to work with or alongside each other. This can create problems, as jealousy and intercompany rivalries fester. Sometimes they get out of hand.

There was, and still is, a lot of hanky-panky which goes on during the 24 hour operations of an airport, and within airlines and airport agencies. Bristol was and is no exception. There are both heterosexuals and homosexuals. There were, during my time, predators of both sexes. This of course results in lots of gossip and jealousy. Many of these liaisons resulted in fights, divorces and changes of partner. One lady was on her fifth divorce in what seemed as many years. I had the misfortune to be asked on many occasions by some of the girls if I could protect them from females who were pestering them!

HR departments sometimes have insurmountable problems to overcome, with the resultant disciplinary procedures, which have to be followed meticulously. There were quite a few other ex-service people working at the airport. The tech's sections and radar bods were all ex RAF, from RAF Locking, which was just up the road at Weston-Super-Mare. The fire section at this time was being populated by ex-Royal Navy chaps from RNAS Yeovilton. These ex-navy chaps were brilliant; they turned this section around from a bunch of West Country plodders to a highly-skilled fire & rescue section which won many awards.

Many celebrities passed through the airport, some very famous. One of the regulars was Cary Grant, who always came in on one of the Fabergé jets (the very well-known cosmetic and jewellery company). He came to Bristol (as I expect you know, he was born there) to see his mother, who was a resident in a local care home. He was a very nice chap and got to know my name, each time greeting me with, 'Hello Gerry, how are you and Lita getting on? Give her my regards'. The film starlets who accompanied him on each occasion were gorgeous!

I had the privilege of meeting many celebrities, some charming and polite, others not so. Some were even so inebriated that they could hardly stand properly or control their language.

I recall that we used to have the wife of a notorious Arab arms dealer, who originally came from Somerset and often came to visit her relations. She used to arrive in an executive VIP private jet of her husband's. She arrived one time with a lot of banned objects - animal skins, elephant tusks etc. This lady was so over the top with her own self-importance that she would not speak to anyone. She had a lackey who had to do this for her. All the banned objects were confiscated by HM Customs. She was livid! When eventually customs let her go through, she would hurry to a door and stop, waiting for her manservant to open it for her.

The last time I saw her, I don't think her marriage to her Arab husband was going too well. She was departing and the pilot of her plane would not board her, even though she threatened him with all sorts! He had received a message from her husband, his boss, to wait, as he was on final approach to land and wanted to speak to her. She didn't want to wait, but had to.

I met and looked after many film stars, sports personalities, politicians, even royalty. I looked after ex-King Constantine of Greece, who diverted into Bristol due to bad weather at London Heathrow. He had to wait until suitable transport could be arranged.

At one time we were swamped by visiting minor royalty from all over Europe. They arrived either by private jet or on scheduled flights, all for a private function being held at Prince Charles' residence at Highgrove. There were about 30 of them and a bus was arranged to transport all of them together.

Everything went off smoothly for their arrival, but their departure was mired by an incident in the departure lounge VIP room. One of the men had a fit. He fell and hit his head on the side of a coffee table and bled profusely. He was travelling on his own and not one of the others wanted to know him or help him, nor indeed did they know anything about first aid. It was left to me to take initial action and get him sorted. He refused to go to hospital and left it to the paramedics who administered to him. Spoilt our carpet too! Just in case you are wondering, his blood was red.

Very often there would be an incident in the customs baggage arrivals hall. Sometimes these could be quite amusing. On walking through the green channel one day I could sense that something was about to kick off. A customs officer had stopped a lady and was interviewing her. She was travelling on her own. She was getting rather agitated with his questioning, and objected to him opening her cases and going through her effects. She was a tall lady with thigh length boots on and I got the impression that she was a lady of the world.

He told her to repack her belongings and asked for all the contents of her handbag to be emptied into a tray. He took time in checking her passport and asked her where she had been. Well, that was it! She started to undress. She took all her clothes off, save for a thong. She had a bit of a problem with the boots, but I resisted the temptation to assist her. Eventually she stood naked in front of him, swearing at the top of her voice and using all the swear words known to man. 'You might as well check everything about me while you are at it!' she said. The customs officer was not the slightest bit fazed by this and continued questioning her. All the time lots of other passengers were passing through; I had to ask them to move on as most of the males wanted a good look. I got the best view of all this. Not bad either! This incident must have scared a lot of passengers, who must have wondered if everyone had to strip off.

Working at a busy airport in terminal management can be quite demanding when you are having to deal with the day-to-day problems that crop up. I was sitting in my office on the ground floor of the terminal one day when the door burst open. A young couple had been directed to me to report an incident which was taking place on the first floor balcony. They were both very agitated and demanded that I should do something about a man who was masturbating in full view of about 50 or so people. The lady told me that he was right-handed, and rather large in the relevant department. When I got there, sure enough he had made a mess on a coffee table and was urinating on one of our new easy chairs. The look on some of those around him was full of distaste and disgust. The man was about 19 years old and when I spoke to him he appeared to be a few pence short of a full shilling. I managed to get him to put his trousers back on.

Word soon got around and a huge crowd of onlookers, mostly staff, filled the area. I was able to ascertain that he was with his mum and dad, who were in the public bar. I sought assistance from the local policeman and asked him to sort it out and please take some action, as I knew that this incident would result in many letters of complaint, as indeed it did. In the meantime I had to get the mess cleaned up and the soaking wet smelly chair removed. Later the policeman came into my office, and suggested to me that I write to this young man banning him from the airport.

I asked him if he had taken any action, and he said no. He said he had found the man's parents and asked them to take him home. I was disgusted with the policeman and later took it up with his sergeant. My time in Air Movements often seemed like an easy life in comparison to dealing with some of these incidents.

On many occasions my parentage was brought into question by a disgruntled passenger or visitor. It is amazing the stories people concoct in order to justify something they have done wrong, or just to give themselves an excuse to air their personal views. In a delay situation, tempers flare quickly and bring out the worst in people, with demands for compensation or recompense.

During my time I witness many goings on. I cannot forget or fail to mention the amount of serious drinking that went on. There were three government departments that excelled in this. I can recall the many times in the early hours of the mornings when I could not wake some of these individuals up to meet arriving aircraft!

One particular incident springs to mind. I was called to the departure lounge early one morning to speak to a disgruntled lady passenger. She was immense! She gave me a serious ear bashing regarding the size of the toilet cubicles, as they, in her opinion, were too narrow. I did suggest that she make use of the larger invalid toilets, which seemed to incense her even more. I thought to myself, I just hope you don't want to go when you are airborne, as the aircraft loos are even smaller!

I received this tongue lashing at the entrance of the departure lounge, where the Immigration Office was. All of a sudden, the door burst open and what might be described as a very inebriated occupant virtually fell out of the room clutching a metal waste bin, which was full to overflowing with what seemed like the previous night's contents of his bladder. He pushed his way past both of us, as well as other startled passengers who were trying to enter the departure lounge. He was trying to navigate his way to the gents' toilet, spilling this strong-smelling liquid in the process. I looked at the woman I was talking to and smiled, which gave her another reason to have a go at me. I suggested to her that if she felt so let down by the service and facilities here at Bristol Airport, she could fill out one of our customer comment cards, and I gave her one. She then proceeded to fill it out, complaining that there was not enough space for all her suggestions. Somehow or other this card got mysteriously lost. I never got my pen back either.

Then there was the case of the Special Branch sergeant who met a rather tasty lady who was learning to fly. She always wore tight-fitting black clothes. A relationship developed. Unknown to him, after some time, the husband must have found out. He could not have been best pleased, as he hired a private detective. The detective joined the flying club, where these two used to meet in the flying club bar and befriended the two of them. Well there you have it - a member of the Special Branch being spied on by a private dick.

The police sergeant didn't score any points with his colleagues when they found out about it. During his time at Bristol Airport, before his departure from this life, he seemed to be on an ever more intensive course of alcohol consumption, and finding out the pitfalls of driving under the influence, which he seemed to be doing on a daily basis.

Whilst on an afternoon shift I received a phone call from a rather distressed lady who asked me to meet her sister off an inbound aircraft and tell her that her husband had died that morning. She said she was not in a fit state or brave enough to tell her herself. I had to gently find the words to refuse to do this.

Another time I was passed a letter from the concerned mother of a young lad. He was about 10 years old, and was terminally ill with cancer. In it she told the story of his interest in aviation and his lasting wish to fly in an aircraft. I contacted her, made the arrangements and met and gave the young chap a VIP day out at the airport, including a visit to air traffic control and a ride in one of our massive fire engines. He was so excited he could not eat the specially-prepared diet he required, which was arranged for him in the airport restaurant. I also arranged a flight so that he could fly over his house, where all his relatives and neighbours had gathered to wave.

It was not long before I had the call from his mum informing me that he had made the flight to the Pearly Gates. She also told me he had wanted to wear the sweatshirt I gave him all the time.

Among our regular VIP visitors was Dana, the Northern Irish singer. She appeared at the local theatres in pantomimes and personal appearances.

I met and saw off a Russian admiral who was the guest of HMG, visiting the MOD procurement establishment north of Bristol; his transport was an RAF Andover, VIP transport. He was accompanied by a lady interpreter.

Each shift was a challenge. Like most busy airports we had our fair share of emergency situations to contend with, such as wheels-up landings, runway overshoots, people dying or having babies, having heart attacks or fits or just scared of flying and refusing to board the aircraft. There were also vehicle crashes, and some even caught fire. Many times visitors from the Continent crashed their hire cars, either on the airport roads or as soon as they got onto the main road, not being familiar with driving on the left-hand side of the road. Then there were the drunken individuals or parties, some of them managing to board their aircraft, others being refused permission to fly.

On several occasions the supply of water to the airport was cut off, so the toilets would not flush and there was no water for emergencies or to make a cup of tea.

Bomb threats to the airport, to arriving or departing aircraft or to the buildings were on the increase, and fire alarms (mostly false) would go off. This resulted in many evacuations of the terminal buildings and the resulting departure delays.

One incident of a bomb threat to the airport caused both concern and humour. A phone call was received informing us of a bomb which had been placed in a new large red post-box at the front of the terminal, just outside the main entrance door. The senior security officer on duty came out and quickly established that he would need more staff to cordon off the approach road to the terminal building and keep people away from the scene. Off he ran to get this organized and to bring in the SOPs for the incident (Standard Operating Procedures). In the meantime the Royal Mail van driver arrived, emptied the post-box and drove off!

Then all these security guards appeared as from nowhere to control the traffic and generally get on with the task in hand. A concerned passenger asked what was happening and was told to move away from the post-box as we had received a threat that there was a bomb in it. He told them that the thing had just been emptied.

There was no way of contacting the driver, so eventually a call was made to his supervisor in the main sorting office in Bristol, so we could work out his schedule. A call was made to his fourth stop, a village post office, where the staff was kind enough to inform him. He then ran off, abandoning his vehicle, and the post office was evacuated, with resultant loss of business to the shop. The airport naturally got the blame for all this.

Passing through the reception area of the concourse one day, I was called by one of the girls who worked for Hertz car rentals. She was having difficulty with two elderly American ladies who had handed their car in after arriving from London. They protested to the Hertz lady that the car they hired was no good and they wanted their money back. They said it was noisy and would not go very fast. Both the Hertz lady and I had difficulty in explaining that although the car had five gears they had only selected first gear and had driven the whole way like that. It transpired that they had never driven a manual car before.

I think I should mention the amount of illness through work-related stress that was prevalent within the airport management. It affected many and caused the premature deaths of some of them, as well as early retirement through stress-related illnesses. Work pressure, deadlines, shift working and long hours of overtime all took their toll on individuals.

This was the era when women were starting to be recruited into senior positions, which resulted in many changes for the better.

I would just like to mention another member of the security staff, a security guard. He came to us straight from discharge from the RAF, having left RAF Lyneham as a C130 Flight Lieutenant

Pilot after 30 or so years' service. He was a very nice chap and I got on well with him. During the quiet hours of some of the night shifts we had many chats about service life. I found that he had flown me in Hastings and C130s on many of my detachments. He even brought in his mess dress uniform for me to try on, as at that time I was an RAFVR flight lieutenant. Sadly it was too small for me.

I questioned him several times as to his reasons for opting for a job as security guard. He said he had wanted something to do that wasn't stressful or mentally challenging. After one of these night shifts, when again we had a good old chinwag during spells of quietness between aircraft movements, he seemed his usual self and nothing seemed amiss with him. Before he went off home he said 'See you tomorrow Gerry'.

That was the last time I saw him. Apparently he went home, made his wife a cup of tea and saw her off to her job as a lecturer at a Bath college. When she returned home later in the day she found him hanging in the garage, dead.

At that time one of his colleagues, a fellow security guard, was suspended and awaiting trial by court. I was a witness at his trial, as his manager. It was rumoured that he had contacted my friend about something to do with his trial, although there was no evidence for this.

The person on trial was not a very friendly sort of guy. The trial was delayed twice. The first time was because a pigeon had got into the courtroom and the officials had one hell of a job trying to get it out. The second time, when the jury took their seats, the accused objected to one of them. He recognized her as his daughter, whom he had not seen for twenty years.

Our friend's wife and his two sons later came to see me and wanted to know about the conversations we had had on the night before his death. All I could tell them was that he seemed in good spirits when he went home. The family wanted some form of explanation as to the reasons for him committing suicide, but none was forthcoming.

There were two other ex-RAF Officer flight lieutenants who worked temporarily at the airport. One, an ex-pilot, was working permanent nights as a contract security guard. In the daytime he was a student at Bristol Dental Hospital, where he was studying to become a dentist.

The other chap teamed up with me alongside my shifts and studied all aspects of airport management; he was with me for three months, working unpaid. After leaving he applied for the vacancy of Airport Director at Norwich Airport, and got the job.

Among those who came to gain airport management experience was a chap who took charge of the airport at Port Stanley in the Falkland Islands. In 1979 a paved runway was set down to a length of 4000 feet and this lovely fellow was sent to the UK to gain as much information as possible, so that he could set up a team of locals who could administer a small airport. Shortly after his return the island was invaded by the Argentinians.

As a highly-trained ex-humper and dumper with the RAF Air Movements trade I thought I had gained some experience for my career in civil aviation. As I have mentioned, I chose to work for an airport authority rather than an airline – I didn't know about anything else. In 1971, when I left the RAF, there were many opportunities and job offers to choose from. I was thrust into a management role totally unprepared for the problems that I and others were going to have to face.

For a start, all the workforce were union members. This enabled employees to hold a company to ransom, especially if there was a need to change working practices, as is bound to happen in an expanding airport.

At this time there was no management system, and no one trained to cope with the demands of an aggressive workforce. There are always individuals who do not want change to any aspect of their daily routine. Just asking an individual to do something that is part of his/her responsibilities can be misconstrued as bullying, which could escalate into a strike situation, together with the demand for additional cash.

When I started as an Airport Duty Officer, all five of us were the first tier of middle management that the airport had seen. Prior to this there had been an airport foreman who happened to be related to several of the workforce. He had no managerial experience whatsoever, yet he was in charge of us.

I soon found out how dangerous it was to form any sort of friendship. Even chatting to an employee, especially a woman, could by some be misinterpreted and used to start a rumour. It took me quite a while to adjust to this. You had to be very careful what you said and to whom.

One of the other new responsibilities I had to quickly learn to master was dealing with the local press, TV and radio stations. I used to do a lot of interviews for all of them. Many were quite tricky in their questioning. Of course when delays affected the airport they would all be there looking for a scoop and continually phoning, especially as disgruntled passengers kept phoning them as a way of protesting at the inconvenience, and of course of getting their name into the papers.

I recall the Vickers Vanguard of Invicta International which crashed near Basle, Switzerland, on the 10th April 1973. Of 145 people on board, 108 died. This aircraft took off on my shift from Bristol, and I personally knew a lot of them. Some were airport employees; others were related to members of staff, or local residents. The aircraft was on a day's outing. When the news came in there were fights with members of the press who kept pestering relatives who had gathered at the airport. It was a disaster that affected the whole airport and the region as a whole.

The aircraft crashed into a wooded range of hills 15 km from Basle due to poor visibility and a loss of orientation during two beacon approaches. The pilot (whom I knew), Anthony Dorman, a Canadian, had previously been suspended from the Canadian Air Force for lack of ability, and had failed his instrument flying rating several times before eventually passing. Before that fatal flight took off I chatted to Tony Dorman while escorting him to the aircraft, and joked with him about his brand new uniform.

In those early days we had lots of telephone complaints regarding low-flying, aircraft noise, deviation from the approach route, night flights and slamming of car doors in the car parks. The list was endless. They mostly came from a group of locals who had formed themselves into an anti-airport committee. I had to take these complaints and record every one. This came about as a result of a meeting of local airport opposition residents with the MD and the airport committee when the members of the anti-airport committee, wanted to know how many complaints had been recorded. On many occasions I would be mentally exhausted at the verbal onslaught I had to endure on answering these calls, which very often would go on for hours. Everyone in the vicinity got to know of the complaints system and until it was changed for an answering machine on a separate phone number, this was one aspect that was unbearable to have to deal with.

Many scenes from TV movies and advertisements were filmed at the airport. There was one time when they were filming in the dark at about 0400, and there were over a hundred actors and extras on site. Many had automatic dummy weapons. As expected, the extras with their toy guns excelled themselves, blasting off thousands of blanks. The noise of these being fired woke up many of the local residents and scared the pants off them, as they assumed that a hi-jacking was taking place. On top of this hill (the airport is 622 feet above sea level) the sound travels far and wide, especially at night.

We told the movie director to visit every house and personally apologize, which he reluctantly did. We also renegotiated the fee for the use of our facilities, which further upset the director.

Things changed when the airport was sold to a local bus company, First Bus Group. Initially the new owners took on all airport authority employees at their existing terms and conditions and pay levels. Exactly 12 months later, when all the profit and loss figures had been meticulously worked out, it was announced on a Friday afternoon at 1600 hrs, after all the directors of the airport had gone home save one, that over 100 redundancy notices were being issued, coming into effect after three months. Jobs on the apron, security and refuelling sections were being put out to tender. There was a proviso attached to the redundancy offer – that if industrial action was taken, the generous redundancy payments, over the national agreed limits, would be withdrawn. The offer was £1000 for each year of service, up to a maximum of 20 years. Fortunately I was not affected. From then on, new employees were offered different contracts and a less generous pension.

I had decided in the years before I left work to make provision for my future retirement. I therefore undertook to up my pension pot through a series of investments. Although I was in a management position, I was paid overtime. These payments virtually amounted to my salary; this came about because of the need to provide cover throughout the 24-hour period. I therefore worked most of my days off, usually on 12-hour shifts, including weekends and public holidays.

At this time school fees were also taking a large slice of my income. My wife, bless her, for many years undertook three separate jobs daily to fit in round the girls' schooling and their holidays, which were mostly spent at our home in Spain.

I had learnt whilst in the RAF that making arrangements and planning ahead for my family and future security was the thing to do. This came about as a result of seeing many others who, when faced with the earth-shattering experience of leaving the RAF and entering the big bad world of Civvy Street, were totally unprepared, financially or mentally, with little knowledge of life outside the protection of the service environment.

# CHAPTER 11

# THE BRISTOL COWBOY - THE STORY OF A ROGUE AIRLINER

During the second week of October 1979, whilst I was employed at Bristol Airport as an airport duty officer, I received notification, via our briefing room, that a Boeing 707 had requested landing and parking facilities for several overnight stays. It was unclear at this initial stage why this aircraft wanted to use our facilities, as our runway was only 2011 metres long (6600 feet) and a B707 needed a longer take-off run to get airborne with any decent payload.

Amongst my extensive duties at that time, I had to advise all necessary government bodies, ie Customs, Immigration and Special Branch, together with our own apron control and refuelling sections and any other interested sections within the airport, of unscheduled arrivals. At that time Bristol Airport was not a very busy place and our facilities were quite sparse, and any visiting aircraft would undoubtedly be a financial asset to our flagging profits.

It was unclear from the information on the flight plan who

actually owned this aircraft. It was positioning in empty from Lasham and had a crew of three, which made us wonder why it was coming at all. So I did what I normally do on these occasions, I sought the advice of the large gathering of aircraft spotters who regularly frequented our viewing area. These guys always impressed me with their knowledge of aviation matters, and if they did not know, they could certainly find out. They were in attendance every day and at weekends there would be twenty or thirty of them present with their notebooks and cameras.

They found the info in no time at all, although they thought the registration belonged to another type of aircraft. They contacted friends who had seen the aircraft at Lasham. Apparently it was an old coal-burning B707-321 which had had several previous owners and was currently privately owned.

The aircraft duly arrived, with many spectators gathered to record its arrival, as a B707 was a rare site at our airport. The aircraft was indeed empty, with some animal pens made up of scaffolding, and the interior stank to high heaven. I met the pilot, a Mr Khan, who was also the owner, and he informed me that he lived locally in Somerset and would like to use our facilities on a regular basis, each time flying in/out empty on a monthly basis, between operating one-way charters from Bombay to Doha, ferrying sheep and goats.

I informed him that he would have to pay cash for all services, unless he had an authorized carnet, upon which he immediately asked for a discount. Which was unfortunate, as he wasn't going to get one. In civil aviation, trust is a costly business!

He did not wish to have the services of an agent for handling, nor any aircraft steps (he preferred to use his own ladder). Only an engine starting facility on departure was required. It therefore became my responsibility to act for the airport authority and collect the 'readies'. He asked for refuelling, which I arranged, and he came back to see me to pay. I collected £5000 from him, although there was an outstanding amount to pay, which he said he would pop back with when he had obtained further cash. In the meantime Special Branch and HM Customs asked to look in the aircraft holds, just to see how big they were (there was talk of gun running, and they had to be sure).

Mr Khan reappeared four or five days later (it was the 11th October 1979) with the co-pilot, the flight engineer and a passenger. He informed me that he would like to depart to Kuwait after requesting a further upload of fuel, which he also paid cash for, together with the outstanding amount he owed. Eventually the crew boarded the aircraft ready for departure, contacting ATC, who then ask me if it was OK to let him go. I confirmed that all dues had been paid and the aircraft started up its four smoke-churning engines. After clearance from ATC the aircraft proceeded along the long taxiway to the end of the runway for take-off. This was witnessed by many people who had come out especially to see its departure.

This is where the story gets interesting. The aircraft proceeded along the mile and a quarter taxi-way and on turning onto runway 09/27 it immediately started its take-off run, without stopping to crank up those four aged engines. It seemed to us observers that it was taking an awful long time to build up speed and lift off. It had gone past the halfway mark and still didn't seem to be going anyway near fast enough to get airborne. It reached the end of the runway, near the A38 trunk road, and the wheels were still on the tarmac.

There was at that time approximately 300 yards to the four-foot-high hedge from the edge of the tarmac, originally an iron fence, which over time had become intertwined within hedgerow. The aircraft ploughed through all this together with its wings, knocking down two 'Gandhi poles'. These were 10-foot-high wooden poles with inverted red painted triangles, to indicate minimum height at take-off. Some of the low level approach lighting also went for the chop.

The A38, incidentally, had over time been raised by the local authority in carrying out resurfacing, and at that time was higher than that of the runway end. It was good fortune that no vehicles were passing at that time.

I checked with Air Traffic Control, who told me that they had informed Mr Khan of the damage caused and the possibility of damage to his aircraft, but he did not respond.

It was some months later that the Flight Engineer (FE) visited us and told the incredible story of Mr Khan and his aviation activities, which came to light following his onward movement from Bristol. Some days before departure from Bristol, Khan had asked the FE to go to Bristol Airport to refuel the aircraft. The FE had refused, advising Khan that this could take place on the day of departure. Khan therefore decided to undertake this responsibility himself. He arrived at Bristol Airport and proceeded to supervise the refuelling himself, but unfortunately he loaded 70,000 lb of jet fuel in the wrong order, filling the centre tanks first, then putting the remainder in the wing tanks. This, the FE told us, was the wrong order for this type of aircraft.

On the day of departure from Bristol, Khan told the FE to arrange further fuel uplift to 152,000 lbs and prepare the aircraft for departure. At this time the FE was becoming increasingly worried at Khan's apparent inexperience. The FE calculated the runway distance require for this type of aircraft with its take-off weight at 7600 feet, and passed this to Khan. The Bristol Airport runway is only 6600 feet, but Khan advised the FE that it was 7800 feet.

It was also noted by the FE that the co-pilot took no part in the pre-flight preparations. It later came to light that the co-pilot only had a private pilot's licence. The only truly qualified crew member was the FE, who had the necessary licences for this type of aircraft.

On taxiing for take-off the FE read out all the pre-flight checks and asked Khan whether this would be a rolling take-off or if they would hold the aircraft on its brakes until full power was obtained. Khan entered the runway, setting take-off power and telling the FE to trim the throttles on the roll. It was noted by the FE that the co-pilot gave no speed calls.

The FE was aware through listening to his headset that Bristol Air Traffic Control had made Khan aware, after take-off, of the damage the aircraft had caused to the runway lights and the hedgerow.

They managed to get to Kuwait, though with the port undercarriage in the down position, as it would not retract. They inspected the damage to the aircraft, which was more than the flight engineer had expected. Metal bars, part of the perimeter fencing of Bristol Airport, were hanging out of the fuselage underside, and some of the hedgerow was embedded within the undercarriage and beneath the port wing.

The FE spent the whole day removing these items and patching up where he could, all this in the Kuwaiti heat. While he was still at the aircraft, Khan reappeared and told him to make ready for departure for Bombay, promising the FE that maintenance facilities would be readily available on their arrival at Bombay. The left main gear was damaged and remained in the locked-down position the whole time they operated in this region.

By the time the FE had finished relating his story, which was interrupted on several occasions by the telephone, we in the flight briefing room were totally mesmerized. He continued by mentioning that whilst at Lasham the engineers there had highlighted several other problems, including both HF radios not working and problems with the aircraft's pressurization, also the compasses were functioning poorly. In total, even before the aircraft's arrival at Bristol, 62 defects had been highlighted, which had to be rectified to place the aircraft in a fully serviceable condition.

On arrival at Bombay, Mr Khan Senior (Khan's father) told the FE that there were no maintenance facilities available to them, and they would have to operate the aircraft, as it was still flyable.

Several flights of animal charters were carried out from Bombay to the United Arab Emirates (UAE). Each time they took off, the air controllers informed Khan that one of the undercarriage wheels had not retracted. Khan fobbed them off, suggesting that they were seeing things. After completing several of these charters the UAE authorities started to take an interest in Khan's activities. His reply to their questioning was to offer forged papers and attempted bribes.

During all this time our friendly FE had not received any pay, and his requests were always greeted with, 'It'll get sorted tomorrow'. Both Khans blamed him for the technical failures of the aircraft's equipment. The problems were further aggravated for our FE as charters of livestock dried up, the aircraft being laid up at Bombay for some time. By now the FE had just about had enough and wanted to get back to the UK, but he had no money to buy an air ticket.

Then in January 1980 Khan senior told the FE to prepare the aircraft for departure to Sharjah. When he arrived at the airport he was surprised to find that Khan senior was surrounded by airport officials and arguing with them. When the FE approached, Khan

Senior made it clear that he should attend to his duties and move away from him.

Eventually they got airborne for Sharjah. The aircraft stayed there for about two weeks, during which there were several arguments about the salary that was due and many other problems that the FE and the co-pilot had experienced, culminating in the co-pilot's departure back to the UK.

Then the FE was told that they were about to depart to an unmentioned European destination. He was instructed to prepare the aircraft for departure and supervise the refuelling, and oddly, specifically to check all the four engines' oil and filters. On completion the FE was then told that departure would be early the next morning.

Sure enough, all assembled early the next day in the hotel lobby. The FE noted that both Khans were present, with their wives, a child and a hotel employee who wanted a lift to Europe. He learnt that the destination was to be Luxembourg.

At the airport, the FE set about checking the landing gear oleos, particularly the faulty left main gear levelling cylinder, which was damaged, the cause of its failing to retract. To the FE's surprise Khan Senior gave him 20 dollars and more or less told him to go to the duty-free shop and spend it. On returning to the aircraft everyone was on board, the engines were running, and Khan Senior was sitting in the left hand pilot's seat. The ladder was pulled up and as the FE sat in his position and got his headset on he was told that they had to be airborne within 15 minutes. The aircraft then proceeded out onto the runway for a rolling take-off.

By now the FE had an audience engrossed in listening to his story and I was scribbling it down as fast as I could.

Some time after take-off, about 2½ hours into the flight, the FE noticed vibration, followed by the No 3 engine low oil light lighting up. He immediately retarded the throttle, but the vibration continued to increase, and within seconds the engine seized. Khan didn't look too pleased. He even looked panicky. The vibration did reduce, but did not stop. Then no. 4 engine was shaking, and again this engine's gauges indicated that it was losing oil fast. It was decided to shut this one down before it seized. The aircraft at this time was flying over Turkey's white-capped mountains at 33,000 feet. The loss of these two engines made the aircraft drift down to 16,000 feet.

Ankara was chosen as the diversion. Breathing was now becoming a problem, as there was no oxygen on board. The two remaining engines, nos. 1 and 2, could not pressurize the leaky hull of this giant aircraft as well as keeping it flying. Then no. 2 engine started to vibrate severely. Ankara was cloud covered, and while receiving instructions for a radar approach the radio went dead.

Five minutes passed, causing much panicking, because they were unsure as to what had happened, and whether it was their radios or something else. Then the Ankara air traffic controller's voice was heard again. The airfield had experienced a total power failure. Fortunately they were then guided to approach and made a safe landing, with both engines operating, much to the delight of all on board.

At the first opportunity the FE inspected the engines. He found no. 4's eight-gallon oil tank almost empty. Engines 2 and 4 would not turn by hand. No 3 was seized, although No 1 seemed good. He then inspected the oil filters, to find that they contained more sand and metal pieces than would be normal. He began to wonder what had transpired whilst he was at the duty-free shop in Sharjah.

After much haggling with the Khans, our friendly FE eventually made it back to the UK and got himself a decent airline to work for. He did make a complaint to the authorities warning them of the Khans' aviation activities. That's where he learnt that Mr Khan only had a private pilot's licence, without any ratings.

It would seem that the aircraft had been virtually abandoned in Turkey. It did come to light, via the Bristol Airport aircraft spotters, that much later this aircraft had been re-registered in Libya.

Oh, and the authorities were on the lookout for the Khans. Some story, huh?

# CHAPTER 12

# INSTRUCTOR WITH THE
# RAF VOLUNTEER RESERVE

❦

Early in 1977 I responded to an advertisement in the local evening
newspaper for people with the relevant qualifications and
experience to apply for service with the Air Training Corps (ATC).
I contacted the local squadron (No 2146) which was based near
where I live, on the Bath road.

I had an interview with the then Commanding Officer, a flight
lieutenant, who informed me that the service was looking for
people like me as most of the officers, SNCOs and civilian staff
within the wing, which covered Gloucester and Bristol, had not
seen military service as a regular, unlike me.

I thought I would be of benefit to this organisation because of
my RAF experience and also because I was employed in civil
aviation. This squadron met twice weekly, at 1900 hours on
Mondays and Thursdays.

I had to undergo the Ministry of Defence security
investigations, which fortunately came out OK. On the 27th May

1977 I received my Certificate of Appointment and became an Honorary Civilian Instructor.

2146 Squadron had a compliment of three officers, two warrant officers and two civilian instructors, together with a canteen staff and a fluctuating group of lads, age from 13 to 20. To maintain squadron status the unit had to maintain a strength of 30 cadets or face being downgraded to an attached flight of another squadron.

I soon got the hang of things and got involved in all sorts of youth activities while training these very willing young lads through the various qualifications that they had to undertake, resulting in badges being awarded. The examinations for their qualifications took place at set intervals, under very strict conditions. With time limits, the papers were collected and sent to Wing for marking. The questions were taken for each qualification from the relevant air publications and consisted of four boxed answers, of which they had to select one with a tick.

After a while, when I had become fully involved with the squadron, I thought it was time to seek advancement within this organization. Mind you, if you had asked me to follow on from my RAF service into the ATC, it would have been a definite no, as I could recall from my RAF service the disrespect RAF regulars showed to the uniformed adult members of the ATC.

There were two options open to me; one applying for selection as a uniformed warrant officer, the other for commissioning into the RAFVR (T) branch of the RAF Volunteer Reserve. I opted for the commission. There were three separate interviews, detailing all the relevant stuff I had gathered together during my RAF service, civilian occupation, personal details and family commitments. The final interview was held at RAF Locking by a board of senior RAF officers who gave me, during an hour-long interview, a thoroughly good question and answer session.

Incidentally I have copies of their findings and resultant reports, which I got after applying for my RAF records of service.

During this session, I was seated in a first floor office facing the selection board, who had their backs to a large window. I was facing this window, and I noticed that during the whole of the time I was in there, naturally pointing out all my good bits, the weather kept constantly changing from sunny skies to rain, then sleet, with the widows rattling from high winds.

The interview concentrated on me as an individual, my hopes and prospects within my chosen career, what I hope to get out of membership of the RAFVR and many questions giving examples of my knowledge of the organization and the training methods with the ATC. I also had to offer my suggestions as to how training possibly interfered with the schooling of cadets. I felt quite exhausted after all that.

Eventually, after another security check, I received written communication that I had been selected for commissioning in the Royal Air Force Volunteer Reserve Training Branch as a Pilot Officer. This was subject to attending and successfully completing a junior officer's course at RAF Newton, near Nottingham. Off I went.

This course was really intense, so much so that the classroom work started at 0900 and finished at 1700. We were then given individual projects to perform and present the next morning, taking it in turns to be the leader. These tasks took up a lot of the evening and night preparing, and went on through to the early hours of the morning. Some of the individuals did not fully complete their tasks, and found the whole episode too stressful. All the time we were there we were being watched and marked for any failings in our character and for the ability to work under pressure. I was surprised to witness one individual having a nervous breakdown while he was there; he was collected up by the RAF police walking around the camp shouting his head off, and not properly dressed. Another individual gave up the ghost and went home.

One of the tasks we had to perform was to give a lecture using the visual aids on offer. These were a blackboard, an overhead projector and a flip chart. Most of the U/T officers used either the flip chart or the overhead projector – I used all three.

On successfully completing this junior officers' course, I later received my commissioning document. This was dated 22 May 1979 and was entered in the *Daily Telegraph* under the military appointments and promotions.

A year later I attended another course at RAF Newton as a flying officer, this time for the senior officers' course. This was even harder than the first! On entering the classroom (which was attached to a hangar full of training aircraft being serviced), I was surprised to see that the blackboard I had used the previous year was at the rear of the room with my drawing still intact on it. The flight sergeant instructor told me he used it regularly for training purposes.

Incidentally the subject I chose to lecture on was taken from an air publication which included the definitions of airfields, airports and aerodromes. I drew on the blackboard the layout of a 'V' bomber base, with its instant ready dispersals at both ends of the runway.

May I point out at this stage that my speech at no time altered as a result of this commissioning, unlike some others. There have never been any plums in my speech.

Eventually the CO of our Squadron left, creating a vacancy to command 2146 Squadron. I applied for the post. Further interviews took place, and I found out that it was not to be a pushover. There were several applicants more senior than me.

Well, surprise surprise, I was promoted to Flight Lieutenant and took over the command of the squadron. There was much to do, in organizing coach trips to all sorts of places, RAF camps, museums and places of interest, even fun parks. The mail I received on a daily basis was astounding. But I did not allow this to disrupt the training programme of the cadets, which was most important, allocating gliding numbers at Weston-Super-Mare airfield and organizing shooting sessions at a local TA centre rifle range. With the help of my staff I also built a 25-yard indoor rifle range. I had on my inventory 12 Lee Enfield .303 rifles, two .22 rifles and four air rifles.

Interestingly, I loaned the .303 rifles out for a while, together with the rifle drill training manual, to an RAF Regiment sergeant from RAF Locking. For some sort of special event they wanted to parade with these rifles, as this type had long since been preceded by more modern rifles. This young senior NCO was not familiar with this rifle at all. I had great pleasure in performing all the movements for him, as being an ex-Boy Entrant, these movements were firmly embedded within me.

The type of lads I was getting within my squadron were superb, and several went on to complete all the stages of the Duke of Edinburgh's Award Scheme. I even submitted my Cadet Flight Sergeant for the position of the escort to the Lord Lieutenant, but unfortunately he came second out of the 10 lads from within the wing who were interviewed for the job.

I had a committee whose job it was to organize fund-raising events held at fetes and other social gatherings, which were very successful. I even used to pay, out of squadron funds, for all of them to go to the cinema on occasion when a suitable film was showing. Trying to calm down their excitement during all these different off-site visits was quite a task, but very pleasurable. There was of course the occasional scrap to contend with, as boys and of course girls are not known to behave themselves when gathered together as a group. But it was generally good fun and I enjoyed it all.

Each year I took the lads on annual camp, but I never really had sufficient allocated spaces for all of them to attend, which caused much upset amongst those lads who did not go. We attended one-week summer camps at many different RAF stations, during which a full intensive programme of activities was carried out including shooting, flying, swimming and night-time exercises and much more. I did get paid for official courses and approved days away, up to 30 days a year. At the time a flight lieutenant daily rate was about £34, which was about enough for my lunch and travelling expenses.

After 10 years I decided to call it a day, as my work commitments and my age were catching up with me, so I resigned my commission and handed over the squadron to another keen enthusiast. I had really enjoyed the experience and took great satisfaction in knowing that I had helped a number of young lads to succeed in formulating their future careers, and helped to make them into good citizens. I was also proud to write out references for some of them when they joined the RAF, or applied for jobs on leaving college. There were of course those I sacked from the ATC. I also got a thrill out of meeting their parents or the individuals who had made good starts to their future careers, and finding out how well they were getting on in life.

On open days I used to tout for adult recruits to join the RAFVR, which was a very hard task to fulfil. I was astounded by the number of replies from people who said they did not have time as their lives were fully committed. This set me thinking to my own circumstances, of working 12-hour shifts, virtually working every day of my days off at the airport and having a full programme of house alterations, including learning all the intricacies of plumbing, roofing, electrical rewiring and bricklaying, as well as taking several holidays a year to our house in Spain, which at the time I was renovating. So how come I could find time? There you go, that's life and what you make of it.

18313237R00134

Printed in Great Britain
by Amazon